Heart Surgery: Excavating, Exposing & Healing the Hearts of Worship Artists

Reyna E. Cruz

DEDICATION

I dedicate this book to you **Lord**-FIRST. It is only because of you that I can even begin to testify what has transpired in my life solely by your immeasurable grace. You alone deserve the glory and I honor your Lordship in my life. You are my one and only, my Father, Friend, Lover, and the best teacher ever. I am love sick for you Jesus-I will never tire of your love for me.

Secondly, I dedicate this book to my children. May the testimony of how Jesus rescued me from myself, transformed me and wrecked me forever because of His love for me always abound in your hearts and minds. Your sweet beautiful faces have been a constant reminder of just how much the Father loves. You are gifts to me. My treasures. May the pages of this book encourage and uplift you as you will see just how Jesus took the life you experienced mom live and broke her beautiful for His glory. **I love you Isaiah. I love you Gabriel. I love you Melina. I love you Hadassah.** You are my joy. And yes…you ARE (all of you) my favorite ☺ Remember to always walk with Jesus as he walks with you. You ARE the head and not the tail. You ARE above only and never beneath. You ARE a leader and not a follower. You ARE blessed coming in and blessed coming out. You ARE blessed to be a blessing. You ARE a victor and not a victim. You ARE an overcomer. You CAN do all things through Christ who strengthens you. You ARE super smart because you serve an super intelligent God. Nothing is impossible for you. You ARE strong and courageous and you WILL do great things on the earth for the Lord.

Thirdly, **Sierra Cruz (CeCe)**. Oh beautiful girl how I have loved you when you didn't even know it. Although life took a turn that neither of us could control, you gorgeous girl have always had a place in my heart. Remember pizza making, cooking baking, craft time and story fun, vacation bible school, snuggles and movies on the couch, our very special spa day and all the memories we spent creating together. God has a plan for your life and He will see it all come together for good. You, precious girl, are loved and wanted and forever in my heart.

Lastly, I dedicate this book to **Richard Cruz III**. We have four gorgeous children and our lives are fully and abundantly rich because of it. Much of what is splashed across these pages changed the woman I was into the woman I am today. Regardless of the trajectory the path of our lives took, I stand and honor you for the husband you were and the father you are.

CONTENTS

ACKNOWLEDGEMENTS

Thank you to my sister, my friend, my ministry partner **Tina Morales Negron.** You have sincerely walked out this journey alongside me faithfully. You followed the command of the Lord to pray for me, cover me, and most of all-simply love me. I am forever grateful for your sisterhood and friendship. "Love you JJ"

Thank you to **all of the students and families** of Break-Free Worship Arts Institute who have honored me over the years as you watched Heart Surgery unfold before your eyes. You studied hard, took in every revelation shared, and applied what you learned to your own lives. This is one of the sweetest rewards to receive-live transformed for His glory. I love each one of you dearly and looked forward to seeing each of you grow more and more in the Lord as you yield to the process.

Thank you **Letta Smith** for your fervent support and exhortation to see the birth of the vision of Heart Surgery come to pass. You have been rock solid in this process of publication and I am truly grateful.

Thank you **Shawan Fox** for always reminding me it can be done ☺

Thank you to my entire ministry team for your prayers, your support, your belief in the vision and cheering me on along the way. **Cereta Johnson, Aida Santana, Danisha Diaz, Daniel Diaz, Mara Otero, Maribell Davila, Liz Martinez**
THANK YOU!

Thank you **Miriam Poche (Mama Bear** ☺) You have believed in me since I was a little girl and I am blessed to call you Mom. Your love and support is incredible! You loved me selflessly and prayed relentlessly. Love you!

Thank you both **Tramona Ford and Mary Buchanan** for always praying and interceding for me. You both epitomize covenant sisterhood to the max!

Thank you to my spiritual mother, **Elizabeth Hairston-McBurrows**, for your guidance, leadership, covering, and absolute 100% pure love. You have loved me just like Jesus. You have walked me through so many areas of healing that will be read across these pages and for that I honor you and thank you!

Thank you **Apostle Theresa Hawkins** for looking me in the eye and declaring "It's a now season for you to write. You have been afraid to write it because you are concerned your heart would become hardened again as you shared your journey. But the Lord says to you on this day…write…write…WRITE! Your story wasn't ready to be released before. You haven't been understood for years by many. You have always been before your time because what God gives you some can't comprehend and criticize you for it. But the Lord would say to you, it's time to birth those books. Don't wait any longer. Write!" This was such an on time word and I am walking it out in obedience. Thank you for yours.

PREFACE

Across the pages of this book you will discover a very transparent, raw, yet real account of my own personal journey through the process of heart surgery. It seems like such an odd title or even can seem a bit brash. Let me assure you that what took place in my life was, is, and will continue to be one of the most difficult yet the most rewarding and freeing experiences I will ever have. My heart surgery process pre-operative, surgery, post-operative and recovery are truly shared on these pages to encourage, exhort, uplift and help to set others free. I have no shame. Christ took that from me.

I did not want to write this book. I told God "No!" so many times I have lost count. I told Him I was good with what took place between Him and I really did not need to testify about it. I am not going to be open and let anyone look into the depths of my personal heart surgery. "No, God. No. I can't do it. What will people think? What will people say? How will they look at me?" Those questions ran through my mind over and over and over again. I was basically plagued with fear and allowed it to paralyze me for years.

So, I began to do what I thought was a compromise. I will teach what you have brought me through Lord in my classes at the Institute and in what I feel are small, safe settings. But the Lord told me enough was enough. It was time to come out of the cave and share my story. He told me, He had prophetic word delivered to me in various ways, He had blaring road signs and wonders placed in front me everywhere I turned, He confirmed it to me in His Word and lastly He sent me an email. ☺ Oh yes, Jesus sent me an email entitled "Are you putting off writing that book?" I FINALLY yielded and began writing what He has given me over the years.

You hold in your hands…my heart. You are literally holding the most vulnerable part of any human being. Without it we cannot live. Without it we cannot function. Without a whole and healed heart we are not healthy.

My hope, prayer, and desire as you choose to sit and read through these next few pages is that you too will experience the redeeming love of Jesus and will allow him to excavate areas you don't want to look at, expose them so he can heal them, and then let him heal you.

Your testimony will shine forth for his glory and you can truly say "I've had heart surgery and I'm brand new because of it. Let me share with you just how Jesus did it!"

Let's think about this time together as you and I just sitting with each other over a cup of coffee or tea in my living room, or my dining room table. Or perhaps we are hanging out in my backyard as we can hear the sweet sounds of the birds singing in the background, squirrels scampering, deer running back and forth across the fields ahead of us and we are just enjoying each other's company as I share my heart and story of freedom, healing, and transformation.

I invite you to join me. Some of it is not that easy. Some of it is tough. Some of it is heart-wrenching. Some of it is painful. You will experience tears, laughter, joy, sadness, fear, healing, freedom, deliverance, and transformation. It will all happen. IF you open yourself up and you are willing to yield to the process of heart surgery.

Ready? Then let's journey together down this road towards healing and freedom.

It's Time for Heart Surgery.

Psalm 139: 23-24 MSG

Investigate my life,, O God, find out everything about me; Cross-examine and test me, get a clear picture of what I'm about; See for yourself whether I've done anything wrong-then guide me on the road to eternal life.

---

1 A LOOK INTO MY STORY

PART 1: I AM NO ORPHAN

Daughter. ☑ Wife. ☑ Mother. ☑ Friend. ☑ Minister. ☑
Teacher. ☑ Pastor…Hold on. Wait. "Pump the brakes Jesus. I
don't think you have the correct Reyna. Me? Do you remember all
the horrible things I've done? Do you remember all of the yuck you
had to take out of my heart and mind? I cannot possibly be the one
you are choosing. I mean seriously if people knew all you had to do
in me they would be so shocked." This is the honest conversation I
had with the Lord about 10 years ago. This was the second time the
Lord had to tell me this. I can remember it as if it were yesterday.

I sat in my living room journaling as I often do and He began to
speak to me. He said "My love, (it's one of many ways He calls my
name) I have made you to be a daughter, wife, mother, friend,
minister and teacher. I have also called you to Pastor my people.
You will teach them how to worship me with abandon and how to
enter into my presence unashamed no matter what they have done in
their lives. I will work through you to set them free, to break them
free, to heal them and I will receive all the glory because of it. I am
not mistaken. I call you Pastor. I have given you the heart of a
Pastor. I've taken every part which was diseased, distorted,
disengaged, and less than my absolute perfection in you and I nailed
it to the cross. You are called. You are mine. I did not make a
mistake. Pastor my people. You will not fit into the mold many form
in their mind when they hear the word Pastor, nonetheless you will
impact the kingdom for my glory and you will lead, guide, train and

equip them for their individual assignments. I will work through you and the Arts to restore them to my kingdom. You will see. Trust me my love. Trust me." And so my own personal heart surgery began.

I was so broken. My life was not what I expected it to be. How could so much hurt, pain, and trauma happen to a person and yet they still have to carry on. It was so overwhelming at times. I was diligently serving in my church at the time, caring for my husband and children, and working really hard to achieve more and more in the workplace. I continued to chase approval. Acceptance. I simply really wanted to be loved, desired, and to be someone who was even worth another person's time and attention. I had no idea what it meant to identify with Christ. God was important and I loved him, but I had no clue what it meant to be in relationship with Him at all. I was extremely driven and competitive. Everything needed to be the best. I needed to be noticed as the best wife, the best mom, the best employee, the best dressed, the best, the best, the BEST. Those are the places I felt the most wanted or needed. In those areas I felt acceptance-even if it was fleeting.

Beloved reader, it took having it all stripped away from me for me to see and encounter the depth and realness of the love of God for me. He wanted me as is. He loved me for me and not for anything I would or would not do. Jesus came at the very lowest point of my life, wrapped His arms around me and whispered, "Beautiful one, come sit with me. I choose you. I want you. You are mine and I am yours." He came in like a wrecking ball and began to expose and tear down every lie I believed about myself, my purpose on earth, and even lies I believed about having a relationship with Him. You see dear one, the enemy blinded me and filled my head with so many distorted views about God it was difficult for me to experience the depth of the Father's love for me. My heart had hardened bit by bit by bit over the years and become so callous from the pain, rejection, and abuse I had experienced that I had no idea how to accept real love. I didn't even fully know and understand what it meant to be loved by Father God. I walked and lived my life like an **orphan**. I had an orphan mindset and carried an orphan spirit which had to be broken off of my life in order for me to fully embrace the spirit of adoption.

When someone has the mindset of an orphan, they have a mindset that is literally impregnated with hopelessness and causes them to accept life situations as unchangeable and they are completely contrary to the will of God for their lives. Carrying an orphan spirit is an incredible stronghold of the mind that keeps us believing we are never good enough, that we will never measure up to be accepted, we aren't as blessed as everyone else, we are outsiders, the unwanted ones, and that we are unloveable FOR REAL. Who could possibly really love US? The bible tells us Jesus clearly says we will not be left as orphans in John 14:18 "No, I will not abandon you as orphans-I will come to you." If Jesus is saying this then it is truth. We make ourselves orphans. We think like orphans. He does not want orphan thinking for us. An orphan spirit or mindset oftentimes will cause a person to feel alone or as if they are in darkness. Orphan minded people also feel as if they have been stranded or abandoned.

> *When someone has the mindset of an orphan, they have a mindset that is literally impregnated with hopelessness.*

I walked this way for many, many years. I knew of the things of God. I knew about Jesus. I knew about the Holy Spirit. What I didn't know and accept was that I hadn't fully accepted my full identity and full inheritance in Christ so therefore I was wandering around through life like an orphan.

There is a story in the bible in Luke 15 about the prodigal son. This story details the life of two brothers. In brief, there was one whom demanded his inheritance early and left his father and home to enjoy the spoils of his new wealth and the other who stayed with his father. The younger son who left experienced a lot of fun and adventure yet he also experienced a lot of pain, turmoil, humiliation, hunger, embarrassment, etc. He realized he was wrong in what he chose to do and returned home to his father with a repentant heart. The older son remained at home continuing to work for and serve his father diligently. The older son, although a part of the family and well loved by his father, carried the mentality or spirit of an orphan. We can see several characteristics of an orphan spirit in the older brother.

1. **Spiritual Orphans are often angry when others receive honor.**
2. **Spiritual orphans are unable to rejoice in the breakthrough of others for reasons such as jealously, bitterness, offense, pride, anger, hurt, competition, or resentment.**
3. **Spiritual orphans relation or attachment to their Father is usually based on "what they do" rather than "who they are" in Him.**
4. **Spiritual orphans detach themselves from those that have angered them or hurt them in any type of way-past or present.**
5. **Spiritual orphans have an inability to recognize their inheritance right in front of them. They have a very difficult time accepting their true blessings which are freely given them to them simply out of love.**

Having the mindset and spirit of an orphan is a terrible way to live and definitely is not what Jesus gave His life on the cross for. To the contrary, He gave it so we could be adopted and engrafted directly into the Father's heart for all eternity.

The bible says in Ephesians 1:5 "His unchanging plan as always been to adopt us into His own family by bringing us to Himself through Jesus Christ. And this gave Him great pleasure."

He also tells us in Romans 8:16 "For His Holy Spirit speaks to us deep in our hearts and tells us that we are God's children. And since we are His children, we will share His treasures-for everything God gives to His Son, Christ, is ours, too. But, if we are to share His glory, we must also share his suffering.

I carried an orphan spirit for so many years. In later chapters you will see detailed accounts of how every characteristic listed above had to be excavated from the depths of my heart so I could fully walk in the inheritance God gave me. It had nothing to do with Him, but everything to do with me.

When he calls you sometimes it appears to be at the worst times or least convenient times in our lives. The call and voice of the Father is one that will draw a response out of you. Either you yield or you run. Trust me-just yield. The latter will just make the process tougher. Believe me. I was a professional runner from Him. I ran because I didn't want to see me. I didn't want o deal with me. "search my heart God. Shine a light and illuminate all within me that is not pleasing to you. Create in me a clean heart and renew a right spirit within me." I literally said this. I also told Him "Break my heart fro what breaks yours. Send me the broken, rejected, despise, and discarded God and teach me to love them like you do." What was I thinking?! He responded. I ran. He indeed sent me all of the above and broke me again and again during the process, but He broke me beautiful. He allowed the refining in order to reach me to minister to woman and young adults not from head knowledge, but true life experience. My own journey of brokenness and healing led me to be able to walk others through their own paths towards healing, deliverance, and freedom. He broke me free to break others free.

I had to minister through pain. I had to minister through hurt. I had to minister through rejection. I had to minister through betrayal after betrayal after betrayal. I had to minister through anger. I had to minister through offense. I had to minister through loneliness. I had to minister through the lies others told about me. I had to minister through financial ruin. I had to minister through turmoil and chaos. I had to minister through sickness, stress, and disease. I had to minister through shame. I had to minister through a divorce. I had to minister through being judged left and right. I had to minister through false accusations. I had to. It is what kept me. It is what helped heal my own brokenness. It is what kept me from taking my own life on countless occasions. The Lord allowed and used every single situation in the process of my journey to shape me into who I am today. My worship kept me. My worship held me together tightly. It was in my secret place I truly found refuge, comfort, and strength to persevere day after day. My worship refreshed me and allowed me to dive deep into God's heart and understand Him as Father, husband, friend, teacher, comforter, lover, peace giver, healer, strength giver, equalizer, acceptance, worth, and more. I could write 24/7 until the end of my days and still not touch all of who He has been, who He is, and who He continues to be to me.

I have experienced and been delivered from every single 'heart disease' listed on these pages. Each one brings renewed freedom, hope, and joy as I allowed Holy Spirit to deliver me over and over.

See, the bible tells us in John 10:10 "The thief's purpose is to steal and kill and destroy. My purpose is to give life in all its fullness." In Romans 8:28 He tells us "And we know that God causes everything to work together for the good of those who love God and are called according to His purpose for them. Psalm 34:4 says "I prayed to the Lord and He answered me, freeing me from all my fears. Those who look to Him for help will be radiant with joy; no shadow of shame will darken their faces." These, and many more, scriptures kept me as He walked me through the path of deliverance. God be glorified through every aspect of my process and my prayer for you is that you would truly open your heart to become healed and free in the areas you need deliverance in. You may recognize your own heart issues in some areas and not in others. Great! Give Jesus permission to come into those areas and heal you. Some of you reading this may be just as sick and diseased of heart as was I. It's okay. Jesus shed His blood to heal, deliver, transform, and set you free from it all. The first step is to admit you have sickness in your heart and invite him to enter in and heal you.

Heart Check Up

What areas in your heart do you already know you need to surrender to the Lord?

Have you ever walked with the mindset and spirit of an orphan? If yes, list the characteristics you want to work on with the Lord.

What changes are you going to make to accept adoption fully through Christ?

What are your personal goals in your walk with the Lord through Heart Surgery you want to see yourself free from by the end of reading this book?

_____

_____

_____

_____

_____

_____

_____

_____

Prayer: Father God, In the name of Jesus Christ your son, I come before you and admit I need your help. I have areas in my heart which need healing. Some parts I don't even want to look at or talk about but I know that I need to. I am inviting you into those places, those deep caverns and recesses of my heart and asking you to work on me. Illuminate what is not pleasing to you and remove it Lord. Search me deeply Lord and bring to the surface even that which I am unaware is in there. I want to be free completely before you and so I yield myself to this process Most Holy God. You alone can do it and you need me to participate. I acknowledge where I have fallen short and am open and ready to receive your healing. Break me open God. I am ready for you to operate on my heart. Strengthen me when I am weak. Infuse me with renewed vigor and endurance to complete the process. I trust you God to remove what is not pleasing to you and to replace it with all of You. Allow my process and my journey to be a testimony for your glory alone. I'm ready God. Shine the light. Shine the light. Shine your glory light through me. I am willing to yield and surrender to your will and your way for my life for I know your plans and your purpose for me are good. Jesus, I am ready.

PART 2: MY BACKGROUND

Mean Girl

I was not a very nice person at all. I was rude, arrogant, FULL of pride and downright mean. The interesting thing was I had no idea. I always had in mind that everyone else had a problem. After all, I was always right.

I Knew How to do Church

I grew up in the First Spanish Free Methodist Church in Allentown, PA. My grandfather founded this church and my entire family grew up in the Lord behind the doors of this old church. I received a good foundation of the bible in my years there, but something always felt as if it were missing. My grandparents were amazing examples of servants of Christ and yielded their entire lives, along with their 11 (8 surviving) children. We were a family of worshipers. You either sang or played an instrument for service and the traditions of church and church service were taught to all of us in the family growing up. I have fond memories of my grandfather surround by all his children and grandchildren at family gatherings teaching the Word of God and my grandmother singing hymns while all the children and grandchildren sang in various harmonies and/or played along on a keyboard or guitar. It was beautiful. I knew all the ins and outs of church. I knew what to say and what not to say. I knew what to wear and what not to wear. I knew how to behave in church and how not to behave in church. I knew all the things that would send you on that fast train to hell too. I knew all the bible stories. I knew all the days of the week you were supposed to be in church to be considered committed and holy. I knew I repented and gave my life to the Lord about 100x a year-especially during youth retreats or definitely after watching the famous rapture type movies in church. Those nights I gave my life over twice just to be certain I'd get to heaven. Although this may all sound comical in some manner, it's not. I was lost. I had no idea what a *relationship* with Christ was like. I had no concept of what it meant to be wanted and loved by God and how worship opens a doorway straight to His heart. I really didn't KNOW Jesus. I knew lots and lots about Him but I didn't have an intimate relationship with him at all. It wasn't lack of teaching or equipping. My grandparents did this very well. My own parents had their method and understanding on how to show me how to live for Christ as well. It was even their best understanding of what it should look like. But, something was always missing. I never felt complete nor did I understand Jesus desire to be mine and for me to be His- completely.

Daddy Issues

My mother married my father at a very young age and had me very early on in their marriage. They did the church thing, my mom served my father like a dutiful wife, and tried her very best to teach me to love and live for God. My father was a very controlling hard man. He felt love was best expressed by providing a home and food. Nothing else was required. I never knew the man who is my father as FATHER. He was just my mother's husband. He never abandoned us physically but he may as well have. He was not a 'present' presence in the home. He worked. He ate. He watched the news. He did church work. He slept. Repeat the next day. He was always locked away in his home office. I barely saw my dad outside of those scenarios. We occasionally went on vacations or day trips but even in those rare moments he was a just a man in my life. I never felt he was a father who loved me, protected me, taught me, cherished me as his daughter or even wanted me in the first place.

The few occasions I would try to venture into his home office for a brief moment of attention that I could potentially grasp were always difficult for me to bear. You see, my father wanted a son. I was not a son. He had a tiny Mylar balloon propped in his office my entire life that said "It's a boy!" on it. (Man those balloons last FOREVER ☺). He wanted a boy and he got a girl. Me. I was reminded of this fact my entire life as that balloon screamed at me every time I saw it "YOU ARE NOT ENOUGH! YOU ARE NOT WHAT I DESIRED! YOU ARE A DISAPPOINTMENT! YOU ARE A FAILURE! YOU WILL NEVER COMPARE! YOU ARE WORTHLESS! I DON'T WANT YOU! YOU ARE INCONVENIENT!" Those are the words-lies of the enemy-that resounded in my heart and mind every single time I even dared step foot into his office. To this day I don't even believe he understands the extent that tiny balloon had in shaping so much of the struggle I experienced along my journey of life.

Again, my interactions with my father were far and few between, however I have very distinct memories I'd like to share which led to much of the hurt, heartache, pain, offense, anger, bitterness, and shame you will unfold along with me throughout these pages.

I had to be perfect. There was no exception to the rule. My grades had to be stellar or I was a failure. If I had 10 A's and 1 B I had failed in his eyes. This drove me to strive for perfection in everything I did. If I could just be good enough and get perfect scores all the time then perhaps he would love me then. This mindset and behavior led me to have an addiction to approval. I had to feel approved by everyone and everything in order to believe I had value for a moment. I strove and strove and strove all the time. I was exceptionally gifted and drove myself to excel in my studies. This in turn did allow me to do extraordinarily well in school but at what cost?

My father would drill into my mind "Don't depend on any man-ever! You take care of yourself and you do everything on your own. Do you understand? You have to be independent!" This was hilarious to me internally because my mother was quite the opposite because of my father's controlling and demanding ways, yet he wanted his daughter to be the opposite of what he was modeling for me in the home. Can we say confused much?

I would lie in my bed at night and tell God "Don't ever let me marry a man like my father. Please God keep me from that. If I am going to marry a man like that I'd rather be a nun!" I would daydream about what life would be like to be loved and wanted by a man. What it would be like to be accepted for who I am and not for what someone else wanted me to be.

I didn't fit in at school. I never fit in with the crowd. I was always the goodie-two-shoes who did everything right and was so perfect. To make matters worse, I was a Latina who excelled. During the time of my youth, Latinas were not considered successful or even intelligent. So to be the polar opposite to what the culture surrounding me was accepting of was always difficult. I was not accepted by my peers including by my own race. I was in this constant state of wanting to just simply be approved. Accepted. Wanted. I battled with thoughts of not being pretty enough, skinny enough, thick enough, etc. It was always some issue I felt I just had to be better. You see, if I could just be better at _____, I would be approved. If I would just do _____ better, I would be accepted. If I do _____, surely someone will want me. Then one day I found a way to be accepted, approved, and wanted.

I discovered if I used my body I could gain the attention of young men. If I allowed them to do what they wanted with me, then I would be loved and accepted-right? Even if it didn't last long at least I would feel secure for a time. I realized that boys were very easy to entice and if I just used my body to my advantage then I would gain their love and affection. I gave myself away at 14 years old in the backseat of a Jeep Cherokee. Real romantic, I know. Oh he told me all the sweetness I wanted to hear. He promised me tons of stuff. I was the only one. He loved me. Blah, Blah, Blah. When he was finished he dropped me off down the block from my house and drove away like I was a $2 whore. Oh and by the way, my parents thought I was at youth group. Parents reading this, please pay attention to your children. Take nothing for granted. Be involved and attentive to your kids. Going to youth group wasn't a safe guard for them although they trusted it was. I am not saying not to send your kids to youth group but what I am saying is you are still responsible to be attentive and in tune with your children's coming and going. Don't rely on the church to do the work you are responsible to do. I digress. Let's get back to the matter at hand. It broke me and shattered me to pieces, but I couldn't appear weak so I stuffed it down inside deep and buried it. The next day we both acted like nothing happened. It was a regular school day. However, what made it different was that now I gave myself away and he knew I was even more vulnerable. He pursued me even more. I gave in over and over again because even though I knew he was lying, it felt good to be 'loved' for a moment. At the time, it was worth denying everything I knew or was taught just to have that one moment of being the focus of a young man. Fathers-treat your daughters like queens. Teach them what healthy love and affection from a father is. Don't let them go look for it somewhere else because you were absent or negligent in showing them what that looks like. Little girls do not go looking for it elsewhere if they are getting it at home. Hold the standard high and your daughter's will learn to use that as the plumb line for their own lives as they grow older.

So, I didn't have a dad in the manner which most healthy homes experience the fullness of what a dad is and I ended up with daddy issues. Plain and simple. How then could I even begin to understand the love of God towards me as Father? He has his ways ☺ He taught me how to love and be loved. He taught me what a Father looks like and how a Father cares for His children. He taught me to forgive my father for his shortcomings and allowed me to see him as His son. He also showed me that my father did what He knew to do. He never had an example for himself and so he simply just didn't know.

I became promiscuous and allowed young men to do what they wanted with me. I was a baby looking for acceptance and love and trying to cure it with adult behaviors which just made matters so much worse. I met a new young man in January 1994 and my life journey took another trajectory completely.

I will never forget the day. I was standing in a common area in the hallway of my high school and I heard a voice behind me say "Hey, you got a man?" I replied "No." And he said "You want one?" My reply "Ok." Next thing you know we were two broken kids trying to figure out who we were and how to mend our brokenness. We only knew one way-through sex. Obviously that was and still is not the way. We just didn't know. Again, I strived to be perfect so I would be accepted by him. I did whatever he wanted or said so that I could make sure he would still want me. It all began on a terribly rocky foundation and we, two broken kids, tried to build upon that foundation. I was pregnant by 17 and a mother and wife by 18. I stayed in college and worked. I worked hard. I had to. I had to be strong and be perfect-remember? I couldn't ever show that it was too much or that I couldn't handle it. No, I had to suck it up and work and strive and strive and work. There was no time or room for weakness. I did well and graduated from college. I had high honors and received various other accolades. I had a family, a good education, a great job, and was serving in church. Everything looked just fine. But it wasn't. I was a broken mess inside. Two months after my first son was born, I received a phone call that shattered my world. You see, my boyfriend (who later became my husband) had been having a relationship with another woman my entire pregnancy. She had just given birth to a baby girl. Simultaneously I found out he had been unfaithful and was also now a father to a child from another woman. I lost my mind. All I could hear being screamed at me was-FAILURE! YOU CAN'T EVEN KEEP YOUR MAN HAPPY! YOU LOSER! YOU ARE WORTHLESS! YOU STUPID STUPID GIRL! YOU IDIOT! KILL HIM! JUST GO AHEAD AND KILL HIM! YOU ARE A WORTHLESS PIECE OF GARBAGE ANYWAY! And the torment went on and on in my mind. I literally lost my mind for a moment. I ran to the kitchen and the hurt, pain, and rage boiled from the top of my head to the tips of my toes and I grabbed a butcher knife and chased him around our home. Did I think about the consequences if I would actually stab him? No. Did I think about my son in that moment who would be left fatherless and then motherless while I was in prison for stabbing his father? No. I was blinded by the pain. It hurt me so very deeply and for many, many long years I suffered inside from the wound of that day. Thankfully God's grace covered me during that time (and countless others)! I never did end up stabbing him. He protected himself with our mattress until my rage ended and I fell to the floor from exhaustion and just cried and cried. Rejection. Hurt. Pain. Shame. Anger. Bitterness. All those seeds began to take even greater root than they had when I was growing up and the roots entangled my heart over and over again.

Along with the pain and heartache I was experiencing I then had to help care for this little girl. Her face and her presence was a constant reminder of his rejection and my failure. Caring for her, being seen in public with her, and having to explain over and over the manner in which she graced our lives was like ripping the scab off of a wound over and over. I was tortured mentally day after day after day. The enemy truly had a field day in my head. The reality was hard enough, but his daily assaults and taunts were excruciating.

Over time, I did learn to not hold hatred in my heart towards this little girl. After all, it was not her fault at all. This process took years to realize. Once I did and I accepted I could not change the circumstances of her in our lives I actually began to love her. When she was 7 years old, we had discussions as a family about having her with us full time. Up to that point we had shared custody with her mother and saw her only on weekends and in the summer time. My heart was actually so full of love for her and I looked forward to having her full time. We bonded so much that summer and became very close. My now husband and her mother talked and agreements were made we would have full custody of her and mom would see her on weekends and holidays for a time. We arranged her room, bought her uniforms for the upcoming school year, all her school supplies, and everything she needed to call our house her home.

Then, the unthinkable happened. Her mother changed her mind. She came to pick her up and my heart was wrenched out of my body as I stood on my porch and watched what had become my princess walk down the sidewalk, get into her mother's car, and drive away. That day forever changed our relationship. Again, I heard FAILURE! YOU CAN'T KEEP ANYTHING TOGETHER! SHE DOESN'T WANT YOU EITHER! YOU LOSER! NO ONE WANTS TO LOVE YOU. YOU FAILED! YOU FAILED!

Those words resounded in my mind and heart over and over and seemed to get louder and louder each passing day. My heart ached and I felt those pangs of rejection once again. At the time I didn't know how to handle those emotions and feelings and I just stuffed the feelings down inside myself. In doing so, anger, bitterness, and resentment just grew bigger and bigger. I put walls up around my heart and promised myself I wouldn't let the hurt of losing her get to me anymore. I turned my pain into a weapon and it was not good. I lashed out on my husband. I lashed out on her as well. She still came for visits but I was so hurt and had built up a fortress around my heart that I became very cold towards her. I thought if I did this I would protect myself and I could hurt others before they ever had the chance to hurt me again. Our relationship was never the same again. I did everything I could to discourage my husband from bringing her to our home. I even tried to convince him at one point to give up his parental rights to her stepfather and walk out of her life forever. I was a hurting, broken woman who didn't really know how to run to the feet of Jesus to ask Him to heal me and help me through this stage of my life. If I had, the story could have looked much different. Instead, I chose to harden my heart so I wouldn't be hurt again. What I didn't realize was that in doing so I was hurting others in the process-especially that sweet, beautiful girl. It took years for me to repent. I didn't want to be apologetic. I didn't want to look at what was. I just wanted to sweep it under the rug and move forward. The Lord did give me the chance to ask for forgiveness though. He always opens a door for us. We just have to make the choice to walk through. A few years ago I received a phone call from an unknown number and when I answered I heard "Hi Reyna…" My heart dropped what seemed like a million miles because instantly I knew it was her. She shared her heart, cried, laughed and more. I did as well. I repented and asked for forgiveness. Although in life we are not as close as I had always hoped we would be, I still trust and believe the God of restoration to do what He does best and that is fully restore what the enemy intended to remain broken.

I walked through various stages of pain, grief, and trauma throughout my marriage. We, again, were two young kids trying to mend our brokenness in a broken way. There are plenty of fond good memories to be told as well, but the result of much of what I experienced through my own choices and what was forced upon me to accept is what I share in this book.

My husband didn't have an example of a father either. He wasn't taught what it meant to a husband or father. He tried to learn along the way. He was always a hard worker and provided for his family in the best way he knew how. We both fell short in many ways in our marriage. I didn't know. He didn't know. I will share more in the chapter '7 Letters of Shame D I V O R C E' but two broken people don't make one whole. Two broken people who choose to remain broken are just…broken. The only person who can make two broken people into two whole people united together as one in Christ, is Jesus.

Work Excellence Award Goes To…

I started working at the age of 14 and excelled in every position I have ever had. To this day I have a strong work ethic and receive favor in whatever I put my hand to. Because Christ has anointed my mind and my hands for His service and He gets the glory. You see, I always had the gifts because the Word of God tells us that gifts are given without repentance. "For the gifts and calling of God are without repentance" Romans 11:29 KJV But now, Christ can work through me in a manner that is completely different. He gets glorified when I honor Him in all I do and I make known that without Him I am nothing. It is solely because of the love and grace of Christ that I can accomplish anything that I do accomplish today.

However, several years ago that was not the case. I had no identity. My identity was not in Christ at all. It was saturated in what I did for a living. Again, I always excelled in every workplace I set my foot in. I worked for physicians and surgeons for many years and soared through the ranks rapidly. I was entrusted with more than a girl at the young age of 18-25 should be trusted with. I ran practices, physician schedules, surgeons schedules, I wrote policy and procedures, I taught and trained people all the time, and I eventually got to a level and position where my head was so big and I was so full of myself it became ridiculous. I never saw it though. It took a complete breaking for me to have my eyes opened. I will share further in another chapter. I eventually moved from Healthcare to Education. I ended up entering into a position in education because of several things that would be quite advantageous to my family. At that point I had two sons who we wanted to continue to receive private school education and taking a position at this school meant lower cost tuition. Although it meant a pay decrease, I was willing to do it for my children. Even in all my yuckiness, I still had a heart to serve the Lord. I went to church, taught my children, served in ministry with my husband at the time. I wanted more of God. I loved God. I just didn't know how to be rid of the ugliness inside and so I ignored it. I sat one day and was talking to God. I was asking Him if I should make this move or not. It was a pay cut and we were living a comfortable lifestyle. Of course in my mind we had to keep up appearances so a pay cut would slash some of the ability to do so. I had very little faith in those early years. I was a facts girl. Show me then I'll decide. This was difficult for me. But I figured I could ask and maybe God would respond. He did. This was one of the distinct moments in my life I heard Him speak audibly to me. He said "Reyna. Go. I am sending you there to teach. And one day you will Pastor my sheep in a unique way." What??!! I said "Oh no, you have the wrong chic. God, you do realize you are talking to ME right?" That was a defining moment in my life. I just didn't know it. This was the first time He told me this. He had to tell me again ☺ just as I shared a few pages ago.

I took the job and my life changed forever.

He allowed the breaking over and over. He had to break me of pride, arrogance, self-righteousness, striving, approval addiction, and so much more. But, it was here in this place for over 6 years the Lord did His work in my heart. He taught me how to and how not to lead others. He taught me and equipped me with tools for business and ministry which He knew I would need in the future. He taught me about what healthy and unhealthy submission looks like. He taught me how to have the heart of a servant and place the needs of others before my own. He used this season of my life to allow the breaking but also to allow the blossoming.

Worship Artists Need Heart Surgery

What does any of this have to do with Worship Arts? Everything! Listen dear one-listen to me. Everything we do and everything we are affects our lives. As worship arts ministers we must surrender ourselves over to the purification and refining process that occurs during spiritual heart surgery before the Lord. All the yuckiness inside has to go. All the stuff we bury deep down inside so no one can see it or touch has to go. All that hinders us from genuine intimacy with the Lord has to go. If not, we not only hinder our own personal growth with Jesus, but we hinder those we are called to lead in ministry. Don't lie to yourself and feel that you are A-Okay when you know there are plenty of areas of your heart that need to be worked on and yielded on the Master's table for him to heal you. There is no shame. There is no condemnation. There is nothing-nothing you have done or not done, have buried inside, have tried to forget and move on that Christ can't take care of. He is neither alarmed nor shocked by what you have hidden in the caverns and deep recesses of your heart. He wants permission to excavate and expose to you the inner workings of your heart; not to shame you but to heal you and bring true repentance.

Heart Check Up

What lies has the enemy screamed at you or tormented your mind with that you want the Lord to tear down for you today?

Are there areas in your life in which you find yourself striving for approval or acceptance? If so, list them and yield them to Jesus.

List some truths the Lord has for you so you can begin to embrace them today?

Take some of the lyrics from the song "You Are Welcome" by Psalmist Raine featuring Erick David Townsend and turn it into your prayer today. You may even want to visit Youtube and play it while you pray it through as you sit before the Lord.

Prayer: Father I come before you in the name of Jesus Christ your son. Here I am. Here I am. I surrender. I throw my hands up and surrender. I may be broken. But you are welcome. I may need your healing, and I say you are welcome. I know you are able in spite of how I feel. I am depending on your Word revealed. You are welcome. You are welcome. You are welcome. Lord, have your way. You are welcome. You are welcome. You are welcome. Lord have your way. You are welcome. Welcome into this place. Welcome into this broken vessel. God I give you permission to have your way. You are welcome into every situation. You are welcome. Yes, Lord you are welcome. Please God I need you to have your way. Welcome into this brokenness. Make me whole God. Make me whole God. Make me whole God. Make me whole God. Make me whole God. You are welcome. Have your way. You are welcome. I welcome you. I celebrate your presence. You are King. You are the King of Glory. You are welcome to have your way in my heart and in my life. King of Glory. Most Holy and precious God. My savior and redeemer you are welcome. Have your way in my heart and in my life. I surrender.

2 HEART SURGERY: NATURAL VS. SPIRITUAL

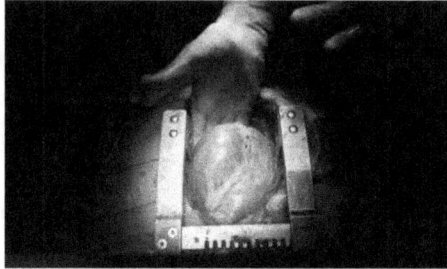

In open heart surgery, the surgeon opens up the chest to gain access to the heart.

Before we continue, I believe it is important to have a very basic understanding of what heart surgery looks like in the natural sense. It will not only you give you a general understanding of what takes place in your natural body, but will help you look at and identify how things can work in the spiritual sense.

According to an article written in Medical News Today on medicalnewstoday.com the following is a brief description of what heart surgery entails.

We will look at the comparisons to the spiritual components in a moment.

*Excerpt taken directly from MedicalNewsToday.com

*What is open heart surgery? *Open heart surgery is an operation to repair a fault or damage in the heart. The surgeon opens the chest to get access to the heart.* The procedure most commonly done by open heart surgery is coronary artery bypass surgery. This replaces the role of the coronary arteries in supplying the heart with blood. This surgery may be needed if the coronary arteries become narrower because of heart disease. Such narrowing increases the risk of heart attack.

Another procedure done by open heart surgery is replacing a faulty valve. Valves in the heart are needed to stop blood flowing back into parts of the heart after being pumped out of them.

A problem called an aneurysm can also be repaired by open heart surgery. This is when there is a bulge in the main artery leaving the heart.

Timeline The total hospital stay needed for open heart surgery is around 7 to 10 days. This includes a day or more in the intensive care unit immediately after the operation.

Preparing for the surgery *Preparation for open heart surgery starts the night before. Patients should eat an evening meal as normal but take no food or drink at all after midnight. Antibacterial soap may be given for washing the upper body during a bath or shower.* The chest may also be prepared before anesthetic is given, including possible shaving. Patients should wear whatever clothes are most comfortable. Loose clothing helps to make the time easier after the surgery when movement is restricted.

It is normal for people to have raised levels of anxiety before an anesthetic. *Patients should not hesitate to ask the healthcare team any questions they may have.*

The doctors may need to run tests before the surgery, such as heart monitoring or taking blood samples.

General anesthetic is then used to put the patient to sleep by injection.

During the operation *the amount of time needed for open heart surgery varies by the particular procedure and the patient.* The surgeons reach the heart by opening up the chest. A cut of 6 to 8 inches is made with a blade along the middle of the chest and through the breastbone.

A heart-lung bypass machine may be used during the surgery. This means using a drug to stop the heart from beating while the surgeon operates on it. In place of the heart's pumping action, a machine is used to take blood down tubes from the heart. Carbon dioxide is removed from the blood, oxygen is added, and the blood is returned to the body.

Who is in theater for open heart surgery? A team of doctors and other health professionals work together in the operating theater during open heart surgery:

The lead surgeon is a heart surgeon who may direct others surgeons giving assistance

The anesthesiologist is in charge of giving and monitoring anesthesia and vital signs

The pump team - people called perfusionists operate the heart-lung machine and other technical equipment used during open heart surgery, along with nurses and technicians.

Recovery *Open heart surgery is a major operation that needs close monitoring and support immediately afterward.* **It is normal to be cared for and remain in the intensive care unit (ICU).** This is usually for a couple of days after the procedure.

Rehabilitation will be guided by the healthcare team, including advice about medications and physical activity. Activities will need to be light at first.

During recovery Tiredness and some pain are normal. Being alert to the possibility of infection is important

Patients should follow the medical team's advice **on wound care and look out for signs of infection around the chest wound such as redness or discharge**. It is important for patients to seek urgent care for any potentially serious symptoms such as difficulty breathing, fever and excessive sweating. Specialist support for activities and other aspects of recovery may be offered in a specific cardiac rehabilitation program

Aftercare varies by individual.

Okay, now that you have a basic understanding of what heart surgery looks like in the natural, let's take a look at some of the steps and break down what takes place during a spiritual heart surgery process.

- ○ *Open heart surgery is an operation to repair a fault or damage in the heart. The surgeon opens the chest to get access to the heart.* Heart surgery, as I like to refer to this process, is how we let God come into our heart, repair or remove the damage, and give us a new one. There is a bit of discomfort, pain, and recovery time but the end result is worth it. Cracking open a chest cavity is no walk in the park. But it is necessary to give the Lord permission to break through the walls we have built up around our heart to protect it in order for Him to do His best work. We are the ones who grant him access.

o ***Preparation for open heart surgery starts the night before. Patients should eat an evening meal as normal but take no food or drink at all after midnight. Antibacterial soap may be given for washing the upper body during a bath or shower.*** Preparing for heart surgery is an intentional process. It is one in which we must mentally, physically, and emotionally prepare for. When we make the decision to go 'all in' and have a 'whatever it takes Jesus' attitude we are responsible to take action steps towards preparing. This may include a time of fasting (no food), prayer and preparing ourselves with the Word of God (washing over ourselves with what the Word of God says about us).

o ***Patients should not hesitate to ask the healthcare team any questions they may have.*** ASK! Talk to the Lord. Ask Him what is going to happen, what can you expect, how to handle the process as it begins, what side effects might you experience, how are you to handle certain situations, etc. Talk to Him. He is with you along each step of the process and wants you to be confident that He has got you. No question is dumb. Our Father in heaven loves to dialogue with us and is eagerly awaiting hearing your voice filled with inquiries and equally as eager to respond. Be open and allow all of your questions to flow freely before the Master Surgeon.

o ***The amount of time needed for open heart surgery varies by the particular procedure and the patient.*** What you are going through in your own personal heart surgery is your own. Your friend, relative, neighbor, etc. will have a different time table for healing and recovery than you will. Each person is different and each journey is unique. You can't compare your needs to someone else's.

o ***The lead surgeon, the anesthesiologist, and the pump team*** Here you have the most amazing team! Father God, Jesus Christ the Son, and the Holy Spirit!! Woot Woot! What a better team to care for you during this process. Our Father takes special delight in overseeing and directing each step of our journey through this surgery. Jesus continually intercedes for us before the Father and He is making sure our vitals are good at all times. Holy Spirit is the comforter and teacher and He is making sure we are continually loved on, filled with power and anointing, and He teaches all we need to know to walk the journey out before, during, and after our surgery.

o ***Open heart surgery is a major operation that needs close monitoring and support immediately afterward.*** Here is where we can see Holy Spirit moving in to monitor and support well afterward. This is also the place where trusted counselors, pastors, accountability partners swoop in to help support in prayer, the Word, and wise counsel as you walk through recovery.

o ***Patients should follow the medical team's advice.*** When the Lord gives us direction and leads along the right path to recovery and wholeness, it is our responsibility to take what He has given and follow it. If we do not do this we have the chance to fall right back into the diseased state we were in before.

o ***Aftercare varies by individual.*** No comparisons are allowed here. Your process is not going to look like someone else's process. Do not become discouraged or dismayed when your process does not mirror that of another. You focus on you and the Lord and allow Him to do what He does best and forget about the rest. Just trust Him with your life, your heart, and your healing. He is faithful and just and he will take you through heart surgery to recovery with his matchless love, compassion, and grace.

Crying Out

Heart surgery, as we have already seen, requires a breaking open of the chest cavity to get to the heart. The act of crying out is a demonstration of cracking open that spiritual chest cavity. The ribs protest but to get to the heart the surgeon has to crack open the barrier between flesh and the heart.

How does this happen? One manner is the act of crying out before the Lord.

The words 'crying out' are defined as: to shout, wail, weep, shed tears to express deep emotion or grief, to 'beat the breast'. Cry-out in the form of an adverb is defined as: to scream or shout aloud especially in pain or terror. It can also mean to be informal and to demand in an obvious manner. Cry out as a verb means to utter aloud, often with surprise, horror, or joy, call out, exclaim, outcry. Scream. Cry. Shout. Yell. Squall. Holler, Call. Give tongue to. Utter. Express. Verbalize. Call out.

The Oxford Learner Dictionary defines cry out as: call to shout or say something loudly to attract somebody's attention; to shout something loudly, especially when you need help or are in trouble.

The bible says in Luke 19:40 "But he answered and said to them "I tell you that if these should keep silent, the stones would immediately **cry out**." The bible also says in Psalm 77:1 "I **cried out** to God with **my voice**. To God with **my voice** and He gave ear to me."

We can see in just these two scriptures alone that crying out is not silent and crying out is not internal. There is an external proclamation and rawness to the act of crying out.

Crying out is:

- o NOT silent
- o NOT passive
- o NOT weak
- o NOT only for us-the Lord also cries out to us and for us

In Zondervan's concordance we see that the word is referenced in three different manners. The Word uses crying out, cry out, and cried out. One of the words is found in the concordance numerical reference 2199 (Hebrew) za'aq or zaw-ak' and it means: to shriek from anguish, assemble, call together, cry out, come with such a company, gather together, cause to be proclaimed, exclaim, shout aloud.

Why is it important to take the time to break down each of these definitions? It is important so you can gain a better understanding and even visualize what crying out truly is and the importance of doing so when you are undergoing the process of heart surgery.

> *Crying out kills pride. You cannot be full of pride and genuinely cry out.*

Crying out will kill pride. You cannot be full of pride and cry out. Pride hinders a genuine cry. Pride gives you a feeling of deep pleasure in yourself and causes you to be haughty. Proverbs 16:5 says "The LORD detests the proud; they will surely be punished." Proverbs 16: 18 says "Pride goes before destruction and haughtiness before a fall." Proverbs 16:19 says "Better to live humbly with the poor than to share plunder with the proud." Proverbs 18:12 says "Haughtiness goes before destruction; humility precedes honor." Romans 12:3 says

Because of the privilege and authority God has given me, I give each of you this warning: Don't think you are better than you really are. Be honest in your evaluation of yourselves, measuring yourselves by the faith God has given us.

None of us are above a cry. If you think you are, go back and reread a few of the scriptures about pride and reevaluate yourself.

A cry is guttural. It is not rehearsed, practiced or learned. Think about a newborn that expresses all of their needs and wants through a cry. No one had to teach them how to cry. It is a response to a need, a desire, a desperation, or a hunger for something.

Need	Natural	Spiritual
Food	Feed me! I want more! I need to eat.	Feed my spirit. I'm hungry for your presence God! I want more of you.
Filth	Change me! Clean me up! I soiled myself.	Wash me clean God! Remove all the filth from my life. I messed up now God help clean me up.
Weakness/Tired	Give me rest! Give me rest, I'm tired.	Help me to rest in you God. Help me to trust and relax in your arms. Help me stop striving. Help me to not do things in my own strength.

Although no one had to teach us how to cry out for these things in the natural, it seems when it comes to our spiritual lives we will fight the process. Pride will get in the way and hinder us from being raw, real, and vulnerable before the Lord. He wants to get in there behind our ribs but He will not invade us. He waits, like a gentleman, to be invited into the process.

David cried out all over the Psalms. Moses cried out desperately because of all the pressure he was experiencing in Exodus 17:1-7. The people of Israel cried out in Exodus 2:23-3:9. Hannah cried out in 1 Samuel 1:9-28. Jesus cried out too. The bible says in Matthew 27:46-50 Jesus **called out** with a loud voice, *"Eli, Eli, lema sabachthani?"* which means "My God, my God, why have you abandoned me?" He wasn't quiet or internal about His desperation. He verbalized His guttural cry without a care about who would see Him, hear Him, or how anyone else would respond to His cry. His focus at that point was desperation for the Father to respond.

A mother knows the cry of her child. She could be in a crowded room and hear the sound of her child's cry and know it is hers. It will cause her to drop everything she is doing and respond. She could hear cries of other children and understand there is a need, but it is not her child. Her response is different than when it is her own child. Just as a mother knows, our heavenly Father knows. He drops everything and comes running in response.

Crying out is a very humbling act. Crying out also demonstrates your need for God and demonstrates your absolute surrender before Him.

Cry out dear one. Cry out! Bare yourself before Him and be real and genuine in your cry. He already knows anyway, but He is just waiting for you to allow Him to come in to feed you, clean you up, give you rest, and fill every part of you. Throw your hands up in the air and surrender. Scream, cry out. Be raw before the Master. It is one of the most liberating actions and you will see Him come rushing in to you in response to your cry. He recognizes your sound. Cry out for an encounter with God. The level of your hunger and the level of surrender will determine the level of response you will receive from God. Your desire is a guarantee to have a supernatural encounter with God. When you are impacted by God in response to your hunger, you will forget about yourself. You will get lost in God.

Cry out and let Him get past your flesh into the depths of your heart.

Then, and only then, can He begin to operate.

Prayer: (This is actually a prayer taken directly out of my journal during a season of deep processing and walking through crying out. I often write my prayers out to the Lord and decree and declare them either as I am writing or immediately afterwards. It is just how He works with me ☺ Personalize the prayer as you see fit.)

Father you are so holy and I am so filthy. I am not even worthy to stand in your presence yet you beckon me and accept because of the blood of Jesus. I am so grateful Lord. Abba, how I adore you. Abba, you are so beautiful and you take my disgusting heart-blackened with sin-and you make it glistening and brand new. I am so thankful. Thank you Abba. Thank you Abba! My soul cries thank you over and over and over again. You are most Holy and righteous. No one can compare to you. There is no one else on this earth, above or below it that can match your greatness. And yet, you remember me. You love me and choose me over and over again. You want me to talk about and teach about heart surgery Lord. All the things that you have given me or allowed me to experience and I can't even begin to understand why, but I will obey. I am the first one. The first one that needs the surgery Lord. Crack me open Lord. It is a dangerous thing for me to ask I know but I know I can't lead well or accomplish what you have called me to place my hand to and remain in this place. Do whatever needs to be done my heart. I surrender. I surrender every bit oh Lord! I will humble myself and lay aside every portion of myself for you. Regardless of the cost. Regardless of the cost. I yield it all. My heart. My mind. My will. My desire. My opinion. My ways. I completely surrender them to you 100 percent. Your heart. Your mind. Your will. Your desires. Your opinion. Your ways. You. You. Just you. I want just you. Align every part of me to you. It's what I want-deeply. Lord, I repent for displeasing you in my response to what you are doing in my heart. I asked and you responded. I repent for fighting you on it. I repent Lord for holding on to what you have asked me to let go of. I release it oh Lord. I throw my hands up in surrender. I surrender. I surrender. Lord, excavate me inside out. Excavate me Lord. Dig deep. I want YOU. I want more and more and more of you. I want nothing left of me. I want to let you lead. Help me Oh God. Abba! Abba help me. Help! It is so hard to kill the pride. I know it starts with me. Kill it Lord. Revive and refresh me anew. Give me all of your heart Lord. All of your love. All of your heart. All, all, all, all of you is all I want my focus to be on Oh God. Restore and heal the areas I have struggles with. Help me to walk in forgiveness when I need to. Help me to let things go Oh God. I will be forgiving. I will forgive and no longer hang on to the pain, fear of rejection, or hurt. I will only cling to you and your love. How my heart adores you Abba. Ravish me with your love daddy. Drown me in your love! I surrender. I surrender. Abba, I surrender.

Listen to "Surrender" by Psalmist Raine & the Refresh Team on Youtube and allow Holy Spirit to Minister to you as you do.

Heart Check Up

Cry out to the Lord and bare your heart before Him. Write out every aspect of you that is hungry, in need of a change, and the areas of your life you are desperate for rest.

_____

_____

_____

_____

_____

_____

_____

_____

_____

_____

_____

_____

_____

_____

_____

_____

_____

_____

3 OFFENSE AND PRIDE

I could have had my face on a billboard next to the words offense and pride if such a thing existed. I've already shared some of the challenges I had to overcome and what a joy I was to be around ☺. I did begin to believe for many years that I was better than other people and that I could not possibly stoop to the level they were at. I did not enjoy being around many people at all. I was a very selfish person and only cared about myself and my immediate family. In my mind anyone else who came into the picture was either a nuisance or not worth the time necessary to invest in relationship.

At the time, I didn't realize it was a defense mechanism to guard and protect my heart from being hurt. I definitely did not like to touch other people or be touched by them. It felt as if I was high above or they were to beneath me for me to allow them to touch me or for me to touch them in any way. Growing up we always were a very affectionate family. Embracing each other or exchanging a kiss on the check was normal. But as I grew into an adult, the barrier over my heart began to push those things away. Pride became engorged in my heart and I never even realized how much it grew over time.

After I allowed myself to be freed by the Lord in this area, he began to show me detail by detail all the ways in which I needed to change my mindset, actions, and behaviors. He ravished my heart with His love and that love drove out all the areas in my heart where I felt the right to hang on to areas of offense and pride.

God gave me a supernatural love and grace for His children and my first instinct when I meet people or am ministering to them is to embrace them. When I do, the love of God floods them head to toe.

I have experienced this time and time again and without fail-every single time-He rushes in and meets them right where they are at. No words even have to be exchanged because the loving embrace of the Father through me says it all. Who would have thought-me? The girl who would never want to ever hug others would end up being a woman known for her embrace. I know the Lord releases healing through my embraces, but it is only a testimony of what He has done in my life and in turn I can share that with others. I am humbled at the very thought of it. Even as I sit here penning these words it blows my mind because I can remember who I was and who He has transformed me to be. His grace and mercy is incredible!

I had plenty of reason to feel I had the right to be prideful and full of offense. I had experienced hurt, pain, betrayal, rejection, etc. and so because of these things I felt deep in my heart I had the right to feel the way I felt and behave the way I chose to behave. What the Holy Spirit taught during this season as He was refining me was life changing. He took all I ever knew or thought and flipped it upside down and inside right.

The word offense in the original Greek is SKANDALON and means: the movable stick or trigger of a trap, a trap stick

    a.   a trap, snare
    b.   any impediment placed in the way and causing one to stumble or fall, (a stumbling block, occasion of stumbling) i.e. a rock which is a cause of stumbling

What does this word sound like? Sounds like scandal or scandalous doesn't it? This word originally referred to the part of a hunters trap where the bait was attached. This word literally means laying a trap. The New Testament used the word to depict an entrapment given by or laid by the enemy. So we can see that in using this word in the Greek the word offense is compared to a trap or a stumbling block. The enemy uses offense to trap you and to cause you to stumble.

Worship Arts Ministers hear me. Offense is ugly. Offense is something you choose to partner with. Offense doesn't just happen. Offense is definitely a choice. No matter what you have experienced in or outside of ministry there is no reason to entertain offense or remain offended.

The bible tells us in Luke 17:1 NKJV "It is impossible that no offense should come, but woe to him through whom they do come!" This right here is plain as day. It is impossible to say that offense won't *come* but it is not impossible to resist allowing offense to enter your heart. Offense is 100% a choice. The bible says in 2 Timothy 3:2 "For people will love only themselves and their money. They will be boastful and proud, scoffing at God, disobedient to their parents, and ungrateful. They will consider nothing sacred" People will be very selfish only thinking about themselves and their own issues.

Paul wasn't talking about people outside the church and ministry. He was talking about those *inside*. So many worship arts ministers (for the sake of the focus in which this book was birthed) are wounded, hurt, bitter, angry-offended. They don't even realize they've fallen into the trap of the enemy. They have literally taken the bait the enemy has left for them and have become trapped.

The key points I will share I have lived. I have learned. I have been through the process of deliverance, freedom, and healing. It is all for God to receive the glory. He did it. I yielded and He responded.

Offense severs relationships. When offense is allowed to enter it works quite rapidly to sever and destroy relationships. It will create breaches and widen breaches which may already exist between people.

Offense handicaps purpose and destiny. Many worship artists are unable to function properly in their calling because of the wounds and hurts which offense has cause in their lives. They become handicapped and hindered from fulfilling their full potential. Most often it is a fellow believer who has hurt them directly or caused the hurt indirectly. The offense just festers in their hearts and minds and instead of relinquishing it fully to the Lord they carry it around and nurse it. I walked this out. I was hurt in ministry. I was hurt by other ministers and I allowed the offense that grew in my heart to get in the way of my purpose and destiny. God had called me yet I was so offended by my brothers and sisters in Christ that I literally gave up walking out the call on my life for 3 years. I let the offense handicap my purpose.

Offense oftentimes feels like betrayal. The bible tells us in Psalm 55:12-14 about David and his experiences with feeling betrayed by his very best friends. David was sharing his heart with God and he felt quite betrayed. "It is not an enemy who taunts me-I could bear that. It is not my foes who so arrogantly insult me-I could have hidden from them. Instead, it is you-my equal, my companion and close friend. What good fellowship we enjoyed as we walked together to the house of God." This was David's homeboy! This was someone so close to him. They enjoyed life together. They hung out and shared dreams and secrets with each other. And guess what? They *worshipped* together. Let that settle in for a moment. Yeah, they worshipped together. This friend betrayed David though. Don't you think that gave David the right to be offended? He was betrayed by someone very close to him and it hurt. The people closest to us: the ones we do life with, our family, our friends, those we spend time with, leaders, peers, share our workspaces with, etc. They are CLOSE to use. Some of them we sleep next to every night. The closer the relationship the more severe the pain and sting of the offense is. You will find the most hatred, pain, anger, and rejection in the people who were once close to us.

Offense tends to be worse to handle with those who are closest to us. If someone isn't close to you or has no direct meaning or impact in your life, you may experience a slight tinge of offense in a situation, but allow the same type of offensive situation to occur with someone who was supposed to be our confidant and friend and it is a whole other story. Only those you care about can hurt you to that degree. You have opened up your heart and given more of yourself to them. You have greater and higher expectations of them. The greater your expectations of them greater the fall or let down you will experience because of the position and value you have given them in your life.

Most believers feel they are unoffendable. Yes, dear one, we as believers feel "Who me? Offended? No way. I am blessed and highly favored of the Lord and I am free of all offensive things and natures. I am washed in the blood. I am sanctified and holy…" Ever have a conversation with someone like that? Be real. It's better to be real and honest and deal with the issues in your heart than to be fake and act the part while you are diseased inside.

Pride will try to hide the offended heart. Offended believers sometimes don't want to admit the offense because they know offense is wrong, they know it causes so many issues so they try to be so 'Christian' yet they fall right for the bait, the SKANDALON. Pride covers the true condition of their heart. When dealing with offense, pride will:

- Make you want to hide
- Keep you from dealing with truth
- Distorts vision (you can never change if you keep thinking everything is fine)
- Blocks repentance
- Victimizes
- Holds back forgiveness

The Lord sees the true condition of your heart though. You can't hide from Him. Even if you feel that you have 'faked the funk' with your friends, family, and those you minister with-you can't hide from God. He already knows. An offended person really believes they are the only ones wronged. This mindset leaves access for the SEED of offense to take root and bitterness begins to grow. Our responses when offense come determines the outcome. How we choose to respond will determine the result we see.

Quarrels and opposition set up traps and hold people captive or prisoner. When a person is deceived he or she truly believes they are right even when they are not. They begin to spew bitter waters rather than pure water. We need to learn to have conversations and discussions that challenge and correct in love and not in a manner that tears down or destroys someone else's thoughts or opinions. Quarreling is really one person trying to prove they are more right than the other person. We get into these situations-quarrel, argue, fight, and disagree but cannot seem to manage in a healthy manner to walk away from the situation without holding onto offense or bitterness in our hearts. You may be strong in your opinion. You may even be 'right' but the fact you can walk away from this type of scenario and still love who you were conversing with shows maturity. Immaturity is displayed when you stomp your feet and pout because you just couldn't get them to understand you were right and they are wrong. Perhaps the quarrel is one in which you feel the need to defend yourself or someone else. Is it worth the possibility either one of you will walk away offended? The bible says in 2 Timothy 2: 23-24 "Don't have anything to do with foolish and stupid arguments, because you know they produce quarrels. And the Lord's servant must not be quarrelsome but must be kind to everyone, able to teach, not resentful". The bible also tells us in Ephesians 4:26b "Don't let the sun go down while you are still angry..." There is so much wisdom here.

Firstly, the Word is telling us not to really engage or entertain foolish arguments. Why? It will only produce a quarrel. Secondly, the Word tells us not to let time go by without resolving our issues with each other. We do not want to be held bound by this anger which we allowed to develop nor do we want to imprisoned by the result of hanging onto anger. I spent years and years trapped by this. Arguments which caused opposition and many a nights of sun setting without resolving the issues caused them to grow and develop into deep, deep roots which began to entangle my heart literally choking the life out of it. God had to break this off of me. He had to uncover my eyes from the blinders I chose to wear which distorted my perspective and vision in every aspect of my life and show me the entangled roots. One by one He began to unwind what seemed to be a labyrinth of offense roots around my heart and I become more and more free with each untangling measure He took.

There are two basic categories of offended people. The first category are those who HAVE been treated harshly or unjustly. The second category are those who BELIEVE they have been treated harshly or unjustly. In either category, the Word is still clear that we choose offense. Regardless if we have or if we believe we have, the option to NOT choose offense is there.

Those who fall into the second category believe with all their hearts they have been wronged. Their feelings come from two types of conclusions:

Inaccurate information: misunderstandings, misconceptions, or 'mind monsters'. (Mind monsters are the stories that we make up in our minds or the torment of our thoughts by the enemy which distorts our thought process.) These types of inaccuracies are birthed out of assumptions. Assumption is the fertilizer or Miracle Grow to these inaccurate conclusions.

Accurate information: the conclusions made come from accurate information but the mind distorts the truth by filtering what is relayed inaccurately.

> *Offense blocks off our ability to reason with logic and understanding.*

In both situations the hurt is real, but their understanding is hindered, darkened, or blocked. Their judgement is solely based on assumptions, here-say, or appearance. The offense has blocked off their ability to reason with logic and understanding. In some instances the mind runs rampant and they have had entire scenario mapped out in their mind to such a degree they believe what they have created in their mind to be absolute fact.

The bible tells us in 2 Corinthians 10:3-6 MSG "The world is unprincipled. It's dog-eat-dog out there! The world doesn't fight fair. But we don't live or fight our battles that way—never have and never will. The tools of our trade aren't for marketing or manipulation, but they are for demolishing that entire massively corrupt culture. We use our powerful God-tools for smashing warped philosophies, tearing down barriers erected against the truth of God, fitting every loose thought and emotion and impulse into the structure of life shaped by Christ. Our tools are ready at hand for clearing the ground of every obstruction and building lives of obedience into maturity."

We must be vigilant in recognizing these traps and stopping them before they are set. We must be attentive and tear down every thought, feeling or emotion that is contrary to the Word of God in our lives. I walked this out. I literally sat one day and said to the Lord "Show me. Show me what's distorted in my thinking. I don't want to live this way anymore. Show me Holy Spirit. I want to see and know right away so that I can take responsibility and tear it down with your Word. I can't nor do I want to handle this any other way. Quicken me immediately when I allow it or entertain it. Help me to be quick to repent and quick to obey your prompting. I can't do it alone. I need you." Simple and real. I was just me before God and spelled out plainly what I wanted to see and asked Him to help me. He responded and over the next few years each and every time I attempted to partner with or allow offense to enter, Holy Spirit would quicken me inside and show me what to or not to do. He's so faithful!

The best counsel I can personally give in getting rid of offense once you have given it permission to enter is to repent and forgive. You take ownership to your portion of responsibility for the entire situation by walking in real repentance first. What does that mean? Well, this means truly having a repentant heart towards the person or situation regardless of who is right and who is wrong. You can't fake repentance. It must be true and genuine from your heart. Once you have given over your heart of repentance, it's time to forgive. Yes, forgive. Forgive yourself for allowing the offense to enter and then forgive the the offender. Let it go and release it to the Lord. Allow Him to take care of healing and restoring you and the other person. Offense doesn't always come singly. There are times when offense comes from a group of people or through an organization we are connected to in some manner. I have experienced offense singly and I have also experienced offense from groups, organizations, ministries, and leaders in my life. Those times it seemed as if the offense was even harder to deal with because it involved more than one person.

In the natural mind I had every right to remain offended with my husband's actions. In the natural mind I had every right to be offended with family members who told me to abort my eldest son. In the natural I had every right to be offended with church leadership (at the time) who counseled me and said it really didn't matter what I experienced or went through in my marriage my job was solely to take what came and move on with life-after all my husband was a nice guy and provided for our family. What more was I looking for? Never mind our marriage was hemorrhaging and neither one of us really knew what to do to repair it. In the natural I had every right to be offended when I experienced betrayal from friends and ministry partners on countless occasions. In the natural I had every right to be offended when after just four weeks after the birth of my first son my father looked and me and said "Man you look fat. I hope you are not pregnant again already!" In the natural I had every right to be offended when I experienced the sting and pain of the loss of friendships I thought would be life-long. All these scenarios-just to name a few-could potentially make anyone have the perception in which I had the right to be offended. But in all reality I did not have the right at all. This took me years and years of process before the Lord to grasp and understand. God can do anything and He can do it in an instant. The bible says in Luke 1:36 MSG "For with God there is no such thing as impossibility." This is absolutely hands down true. However, God is a gentleman. He will not force Himself on anyone. He likes to be invited in.

So, you see dear one, it wasn't that God couldn't just rescue me and deliver me immediately because He could have. I, me, I had to make the choice to hand over the areas of my heart one by one which needed mending and healing.

Holy Spirit continued to teach me how to walk with discernment to see offense coming, then to prostrate myself before the Lord in prayer giving it all over to Him, and to carry on with my journey knowing in my heart I was free from offense. I will be completely honest and transparent. Some days were harder than others. There were times it was a daily encounter, or a minute by minute encounter, or hour by hour, or week by week, or month by month encounter with the spirit of offense, but He never left me or forsook me. He never left me alone. He was always right there beside me holding my hand through each step.

The Word and worship held me together. All the moments I wanted to give up and throw my hands in the air and shout 'forget this!', the Lord would beckon me every so softly and say "Beautiful one, come sit with me. Let me refresh you and restore you. Come. Come into my chamber and allow me to strengthen you with my presence. Just worship Me. Release it all in your worship before me. You will see when you throw yourself into worship with reckless abandon, I come swooping in to rescue you my love." And so I did. Each and every time I would find myself desperate to run into His presence. There were times when I felt I couldn't get to Him fast enough. I would literally lock myself in a small closet I had in my bedroom and just be with him. I would sit

> *The Word and worship held me together.*

and just dump out on Jesus everything I had experienced that day and then once I did that, I would begin to worship Him simply because I loved Him and I knew He loved me. I wasn't necessarily looking for answers or a quick fix. I was looking for a safe place to be ME. A place to be loved just as I am-flaws and all. Then my heart would swell with gratitude for His immense love for me and I would just begin to worship. My pain and experiences throughout my entire process of refining drove me deeper and deeper into worship before Him. It was in THAT place where I was closest to Him and I knew He was for me. It was also in THAT place where I would receive correction and direction on how to move forward. Some of the things the Lord would ask me to do were not easy and I didn't want to do them, but I feared the Lord more than I feared the task before me.

What kinds of tasks you might be wondering? Well, for instance, going to someone and asking for forgiveness from them when I knew they did me wrong yet I humbled myself to ask them to forgive me for causing hurt, pain, or strife. There were moments I had to swallow my pride and go before my husband and repent for what I had said or done in retaliation for how I felt he behaved or treated me. I also on one occasion had to minister before and to someone who had wounded me deeply in ministry.

The Lord had already prepared me that I would have to do this one day but I never knew when it would happen. I was totally caught off guard at a conference myself and this other minister were attending. I had no idea she was even there. There came a point in the activations which were taking place where we had to form two circles. One circle needed to face inward and the other circle needed to face outward. Prophetic song was played and we were instructed to minster in prophetic movement to the person in front of us. After several minutes the conference leaders announced the inside circle should take two steps the left. Now, whoever remained in front of us at this point, we were to minister to. This went on for several minutes. Minister. Step to the side. Minister. Step to the side. Minster. Step to the side. Minister. BAM! Who ended up right in front of me? You guessed it. The young woman who had hurt me deeply was right in front of my face. Holy Spirit said to me 'I told you. You are more ready for this moment than you know. I have prepared you. Now, allow me to minister through you.' So, I obeyed. She was just as stunned as I was. I could see it in her face. I obeyed the Lord and silently prayed 'Have your way. Do what you want Holy Spirit'. I ministered to her and at the very point in the song playing where prophetic decrees were being sung about forgiveness and healing. There was so much more to what was being sung but those two things stuck out to me most. She broke down and began to sob and sob. She looked straight into my eyes and I know she saw eyes of love staring right back at her because Christ was shining in that moment. Reyna was yielded to allow Him to do the work. The exercise ended right after I had ministered to her. She threw her arms around my neck and squeezed me so hard. She kept saying "I'm sorry. Forgive me. I'm sorry. I'm sorry. You didn't deserve what I chose to do. You are the real deal. I saw your heart through your eyes and you are the real deal." With that, I returned her embrace and simply whispered 'I forgive you'. I didn't see her for the remainder of the conference. Trust me, I looked for her ☺. I believe to this day the Holy Spirit orchestrated that very moment for her to receive and see what she hadn't seen before, but more for me to yield, obey and grow from the experience. I can't talk to you or anyone else about letting go of offense, forgiveness, or yielding to the process of hard things if I myself haven't done it. I've learned to allow the process. It will be good.

The bible says in Isaiah 41:10 "Don't be afraid, for I am with you. Do not be dismayed, for I am your God. I will strengthen you. I will help you. I will uphold you with my victorious right hand." Also in Isaiah 43:1b-2,4b it says "I have called you by name; you are mine. When you go through deep waters and great trouble, I will be with you. When you go through rivers of difficulty you will not drown!

When you walk through the fire of oppression, you will not be burned up; the flames will not consume you…because you are precious to me. You are honored, and I love you." These scriptures kept me focused. He washed me with His Word continually. He reminded me everyday with these two scriptures that He was with me through every moment.

Offense truly is a by-product or manifestation of pain in someone's life. Our next chapter together will address pain, but it is important for you to know here at this moment that offense can be manifested due to pain a person experiences. The offense begins to behave like a safe guard around the person's heart. It is not healthy at all, but the person's pain embraces offense and it becomes A FENCE around their heart. It will block out all emotion and feeling and keep the pain inside. The pain is nurtured and nursed and coddled. It is almost protected so much so that the person has a difficult time becoming free as they have grown so accustomed to living this way.

Offended people oftentimes are the ones who always expect the worst outcome in EVERY situation. When a person is severely offended or has held on to offense as a way of life for long periods of time you will begin to see them react out of that place for everything. No matter how big or how small a situation may be, the offended person will blow it completely out of proportion and declare all the negative that can happen. Negativity becomes a part of their personality. For example, you are rushing into a service because you are running a bit late and you are responsible for getting the communion elements together. It's only your second time handling this task and you want to make sure you are present and ready to serve. The kids woke up late and the dog ran away and you just simply are running behind. Sister Sally who has a tendency to become easily offended all the time for everything is in the lobby and you didn't have time to stop and greet her. You simply pass her bye with a quick wave hello and continue to your post. Sister Sally has now fashioned in her mind that you don't like her because you didn't stop to say hello. She thinks you are definitely telling all the other woman in the church to stay away from her and now she will have no friends in church. She determines she will be all alone in the world and will end up leaving the church because no one will talk to her anymore. She pictures herself all alone in her bedroom with violin music playing in the background and a box of doughnuts on her bed calling her name to numb the pain. Meanwhile you are preparing the communion elements for service, but have the thought to check on Sister Sally afterwards because you want to invite her over for dinner sometime but just didn't have the time at that moment to stop and do so.

Ok, seriously I realize it's a bit drastic but it is not as far fetched as it seems. There are many scenarios like these that offended people make up in their minds. The fantasy they create in their minds becomes such a reality to them because their mindset and vision is distorted by the lens of offense. I've been there. Done that.

The bible tells us in Psalm 119:165 "Allow the Word of God to be the equalizer to your responses." This is quite clear. Measure everything against the Word of God. If it doesn't line up to the Word or to the characteristics of Christ then discard it completely.

Offended people feel as if they have never been the victimizer but only the victim. This type of scenario is one in which an offended person will really convince themselves and try to convince others they have NEVER been on the other side of stone throwing. They will play the role of victim and portray they are the ones always being rightfully offended but never the offender. All too quickly we can find out the truth about them, you, and anyone in moments by reviewing a few simple items:

What are your text messages saying?

What are your inner thoughts and dialogues saying?

What is your pillow talk like with your mate?

What are you looking for when you become a Facebook troll for the night and even try to 'throw shade' indirectly to others?

Psalm 139:23-24 "Search me O God…shine a spotlight on my heart…" Really? Do you really want Him to? What is He going to find in there?

The bible says in Proverbs 19:11 for us to be slow to anger, and to [have] the glory to overlook an offense. This scripture is telling us clearly to pump our breaks on our responses and reactions and overlook an offense. Don't be a self-proclaimed victim. Squash that victim mentality today!

Offense grows in our lives because it has become a subject of our meditation. Now, I am not talking about or referring to the concept of New Age meditation practices. I am talking about biblical meditation.

Meditation means to think upon, to review over and over and over in your mind, to rehearse.

The bible says to meditate on His laws and precepts "for as a man thinketh so is he". Proverbs 23:7

Offended people meditate on things such as:

- I think I am right
- He/She is wrong
- They did me dirty
- They hurt me
- It's not fair
- I remember EXACTLY what he/she said and did to me

The bible says in Joshua 1:8 "Study this book of the law continually. <u>Meditate</u> on it day and night so you may be sure to obey all that is written in it."

Psalm 1:2 says "But they delight in doing everything the Lord wants; day and night they think about His law"

Psalm 19:14 says "May the words of my mouth and the thoughts [meditations] of my heart be pleasing to you, O lord, my Rock and my Redeemer."

Psalm 48:9 says " O God, we meditate on your unfailing love as we worship in your temple."

Psalm 119:97 says "O how I love your law! I think about it all day long."

Misguided meditations or rehearsing scenarios of offense and offenders steals your peace. The bible says in Colossians 3:16-17a "Let the peace that comes from Christ rule in your hearts. For as members of one body you are called to live in-peace. And, always be thankful. Let the words of Christ, in all their richness, live in your hearts and make you wise."

What you meditate on will manifest itself in you life. Do you want to meditate on offense and offenders or do you want to meditate on the life giving Word of God in order to see that manifest in your life?

Oftentimes offended people live a lifestyle of offense.
Everybody, everywhere, everything offends the offense.

When you are filled with the Holy Spirit and you yield your life to Him truly you cannot avoid truth. Truth shines light on all situations. So when you are in worship, prayer and fellowship you must do a self check and ask yourself "is the Spirit of Truth present? Or are you allowing the spirit of offense operating and manifesting a lie to yourself and others to be present?

Where the Spirit of the Lord is there is freedom. Freedom means free. There is no offense, pain, anger, or bondage in freedom.

True worshipers will worship in spirit and in truth. The bible says in John 4:23-24 MSG "It is who you are and the way you live that count before God. Your worship must engage your spirit in the pursuit of truth. That's the kind of people the Father is out looking for. Those who are simply and honestly themselves before Him in their worship. God is sheer being-itself spirit. Those who worship Him must do so out of the very beings, their true selves in adoration."

> *Truth will always overrule lies.*

Truth overrules lies. Offense can also be considered or compared to a web. The offense builds a web of lies preconceived in your own mind which were birthed out of your own meditations on the offense.

As a worship arts minister imagine you are literally bound in chains, your garments are soiled and you are emitting a stench from your body. You are this way because you are walking around offended. You are presenting this to a most Holy God and leading others in the same manner. You are not offering this up to the Lord for cleansing and out of a heart of repentance but as a form of defiled worship because an offended heart is full of pride and thinks nothing is wrong with them at all. Wrong! Just yield and let it go. Lift those hands and give your heart over to the Lord and let Him have His way to heal you. Don't keep defiling the altar with your carrying of offense.

Even if you need to step down off that altar and go to whomever has offended you or to whom you have offended-do it. The bible is clear in telling us in Matthew 5:24 "Leave your sacrifice there at the altar. Go and be reconciled to that person. Then come and offer your sacrifice to God." Beloved, it's worth it. Let it go. Reconcile with your brother or sister and then go back to the altar for the Lord to heal and restore you.

Pure purposeful worship creates an atmosphere of repentance, humility, and forgiveness. If you can go before a Holy God and not have a heart change, a mindset shift, a true breaking towards freedom you are not really worshipping-at least not the one true God. Some other form or type of spirit is operating. There is no way a yielded heart in the presence of God can remain unchanged.

You can dance and shout and pray in tongues all day long. You can become slain in the spirit and slathered in so much oil you slip and slide right out of service, but if you are STILL mad, hurt, offended, holding resentment and pain, you were not talking with God. His very presence carries love, healing, forgiveness, restoration, wholeness and freedom. You can't be in His presence and leave unchanged. It's impossible.

You CAN be PRESENT like a fixture and not encounter His presence when you are disconnected or disengaged because offense will block truth from flowing through you.

Worship arts ministers, you are a conduit of good or bad. You can either release truth and freedom or you can release lies and bondage.

When you surrender your heart of offense to the Master surgeon to remove you can sing, dance, paint, write, create, and play your way to breakthrough. This all comes with a yielded heart that's says ENOUGH! "I'm broken God but you take the brokenhearted and place them in families. I'm hurting God but you bind up (heal) the broken hearted. I'm scared God but your perfect love casts out fear. I'm mad but I won't let anger gain control over me. I will not let the sun go down on my anger. I'll be strong and courageous for you tell me do not fear. I'm in pain and I'm offended God but you said its impossible offense won't' come but I keep my eyes on you alone. You keep in perfect peace those whose eyes are stayed on you."

> *If you are truly worshipping in spirit and in truth God will address your heart in that moment and will correct you for your good.*

If you are truly worshiping in spirit and truth God will address your heart in that moment and He will correct you for your good. He will take what the enemy meant for evil to trap you in skandalon and turn it into good IF you surrender.

Offense also tends to rehearse (meditates) responses. Most of us will have a whole scenario mapped out in our minds ready for when we see our offender (victimizer). However, when we are meditating (rehearsing) on the Word of the living God our response is one filled with truth and life and not one we spew with ill intentions or even the extreme of hatred towards another person. Worship exposes us. It's a place of absolute nakedness before God. We can't hide a thing. So, if you want to stay offended you won't worship. You won't yield yourself to the processing. Yield yourself to the purpose being birthed behind the pain of offense.

When our hearts are not fully given over in worship we are allowing and giving permission to Satan to be at work in us. Sound harsh? Well, dear one, it's in the Word of God. Ephesians 2:2 tells us "Satan, the mighty prince of the power of the air is the spirit at work in the hearts of those who refuse to obey God." If you hold onto offense, anger, pain, pride, etc. you are refusing to obey God.

Stop for a moment. Close your eyes and ask the Lord to shine a spotlight on your heart and illuminate where you may have hidden offense deep inside. Now, yield to His hand at work in you. Give it to him. Every person, every situation, every place, every group, everything, every aspect. Give it to Him and be free!

Heart Check Up

What areas of your life have you held onto offense?

Who has offended you and why do you feel offended?

Who do you know you have offended and why did you choose to behave in the manner you did?

Is their pride in your heart keeping you from being repentant?

_____

_____

_____

_____

_____

_____

_____

_____

_____

Prayer: Father, in the name of Jesus Christ your son I sit here with you and ask you to illuminate what is in my heart that is not pleasing to you in the area of offense. Forgive me Lord for offending you first. In every area of my life which has been displeasing to you or grieved your heart I repent and ask for and welcome your forgiveness today. Show me Lord who I may have offended knowingly or unknowingly and also show me Lord the offense I've allowed to grow and develop in my own heart. I desire repentance, reconciliation, and restoration in all my relationships Lord. If I have offended in my own home with my family-forgive me. If I have offended in the workplace, in church, in ministry, in my friendships, and in my interactions in everyday life with people I may never meet again-forgive me. Open my heart Lord and begin excavating all that is not pleasing to you. I give you permission to come in and do what is necessary to take me to a place of true repentance and forgiveness. I want to be free. I want to be whole. I want to be more like you Jesus. Help me to keep my eyes on you each and every day. I embrace your peace. I embrace your love. I embrace your forgiveness and healing. By the power of the blood shed on the cross by you Jesus for me I declare the severing of my partnership with the spirit of offense today. I no longer walk offended and I no longer offend. I walk with the love and peace of God and emulate your character Jesus in my daily living. I declare freedom in my heart and renewed freedom in my worship. You are a good and gracious Father and I thank you for bathing me in your love. In Jesus precious name, Amen.

My Journey of Worship

4 PAIN

Pain-Yeah Let's Go there. In this chapter, we are going to address pain. I have highlighted several attributes of pain and also areas the Lord had to teach me about myself to deliver me.

I experienced tremendous amounts of pain in my life. I know the hurt of betrayal. I know the pain of adultery. I know the pain of addiction. I know the hurt of rejection. I know the pain of abandonment. I know the hurt of judgement. I know the pain of shame. I know the excruciating hurt of divorce. I know the pain of scandal. I know. Dear one, beloved reader you are not alone. However, don't stay in the place of embracing pain. Don't nurture pain and coddle pain or allow pain to be a comfortable resident in your heart. There is freedom in evicting pain and hurt from your heart and your life.

There is always purpose in the pain we experience in life.
Nothing takes the Lord by surprise and He can and will get glory out of the pain we all have to experience. Pain drives us closer to the cross and causes us to dig deeper into the heart of God. ***Psalm 119:71 says "The suffering you sent was good for me, for it taught me to pay attention to your principles."*** The bible also tells us in ***Romans 8:28 "And we know that God causes everything to work together for the good of those who love God and are called according to his purpose for them."*** Pain isn't fun nor do we enjoy experiencing it. However, there is purpose in the pain we do experience.

Letting go of pain is a choice. We have to make the effort to choose to let it go. Some people don't want to be healed. Some people don't really want to be set free. There are people who choose to remain broken and remain fractured to a degree because it will then give them an excuse for their behavior.

I had all the reasons in the world to feel I had the right to remain in my pain and felt my behavior was okay because of it. Many of us will fight the process of being healed from pain because the process of healing requires us to yield or surrender completely. It makes us look in the mirror at ourselves and admit what we would rather not talk about. Those who do not want to yield to this part of the process will oftentimes react towards those trying to help them in such a strong manner because they are afraid to face the pain dead on. They may even be comfortable in their dysfunction. It can sadly become a normalcy and many train themselves to just live with it. I experienced this first hand. There was a time when I was confronted with this reality and those who tried to reach me in the manner they thought was best caused me to react out dramatically because I had fear of facing the pain. I didn't want to feel anything. I thought I was just fine the way I was and had created an environment in which I was completely comfortable in the dysfunction of my life. Pain was a prison I allowed myself to live in. No one put me there. I sent myself there. I could have let it go and surrendered it all at the feet of Jesus, but the enemy lied to me and had me convinced I was safer inside the prison on my mind and if I even attempted to break out I would just get hurt all over again. Being behind the prison bars of my mind kept me safe. Did it really? No, it kept me in bondage. It kept me saturated in continual pain which became so normal I couldn't even really think about what life would be like free from it.

I heard a story told once which was quite comical but when you really catch the moral of the story you realize how much you personally control your environment, your choices, and their effects. Again, you are responsible for what you choose to remain in pain about.

> *There were two friends who worked together on a construction site. Each of them took lunch together at the same time every day. Jim always had a bologna sandwich for lunch every day. Norman had a salad some days, a sandwich another day, or perhaps some leftovers on yet another day. Each day they ventured out to lunch together and followed the same routine. One day after several weeks of this, Jim opened his lunch box to get ready for lunch and became furious by what he found. Another bologna sandwich. He was so tired of eating this bologna sandwich every single day and began to rant and rave about just how tired of it he was. Norman was caught off guard and quite surprised at this behavior and asked Jim if he was okay. "No I am not okay! I am so tired of eating this bologna sandwich every single day! I am sick of it!" Norman paused quietly for a moment and then responded, "Well have you shared this information with your wife. Perhaps she will pack you something different for lunch if you just let her know that you want something different." Jim spun around and glared at Norman and exclaimed "What are you talking about? I pack my own lunch every day!"*

Jim had total control over the choices he made every day with his lunch. Yet, he was angry and frustrated and basically took it out on Norman simply because he chose to pack the same lunch every day. He made the choice and he was in control of changing it. He chose to stay in the same behavior daily and got the same result. He got mad and frustrated, however, it was due to his own choice not to make a change and pack something different.

Pain can be generational. There are learned behaviors and learned responses which occur simply because it is what has been modeled for us or taught to us through our family. For example, growing up I learned to be impatient, judgmental, rude, and even at times manipulative because I watched family members operate in this manner. They were only behaving that way because they had experienced hurt or pain in their past and now had defense mechanisms and walls built up to protect their hearts that were displayed in the attributes listed above. I, in turn, learned these behaviors and emulated them quite often. When I felt my own personal pain or hurt these responses would become amplified as I was now projecting my own emotions coupled with what I had learned. It became a generational issue for me which had to be broken off of my life. The only way this could take place was by learning to measure my character, responses, feelings and emotions with the Word of God. This is a tough challenge for many of us. As soon as we take the Word to challenge and measure, the reaction or response can be fierce. The Word of God is ... *"alive and powerful. It is sharper than the sharpest two-edged sword, cutting between soul and spirit, between joint and marrow. It exposes our innermost thoughts and desires." Hebrews 4:12* The Word is going to cut right through and you can either embrace it and accept the process or fight it. What is the alternative? You can measure things against your own ideas, feelings, familial ways and mannerisms and you will always find an excuse or <u>feel</u> as if you are right, but when you measure by the Word of God the light of truth will illuminate the darkness and expose your heart.

Pain is responsible for all addictive behaviors. Everyone is affected in a different manner and not all experiences of pain lead to addictions. Catch what I am saying at this point. However, all addictive behaviors stem from some type of pain. Several types of addictions are: drugs, drinking, compulsions, perfectionism, approval, eating, etc. I personally struggled the most with the latter three listed. I was driven to perfectionism because of all I experienced as a child. I just had to be perfect. I needed approval and it became an addiction. When I did receive it, I still needed more and more. The addiction never satisfies. I also ate to drown my pain. There was a time I was nearly 200 pounds. A 5'1 female should not equal 200 pounds but I did. At that point in my life, I had reached a low in my emotional and spiritual well -being and my highest weight. I ate when I was happy, sad, mad, frustrated, angry, and lonely. You name it and I would find a reason to eat excessively. It was euphoric and for a moment I didn't think about what hurt me the most. I was just able to enjoy the food. Instead of running into the arms of Jesus with my pain and my hurt, I ran to people to approve me and man to feed me. I also suffered with an addictive behavior that required me to use my body in degrading manners. I felt if I did these things I wouldn't have to feel the pain of rejection. If I allowed myself to be thought of as the best in a bedroom, whether I agreed with what took place or not, then I would be affirmed and approved. I became numb to the pain internally and externally which I experienced on a regular basis. Although I experienced this numbness I was still addicted to the thought of being approved. It was not the actions I chose to participate in which made me chase more. It was the response of what I associated with approval that made the pain bearable. I made the choice. I was responsible for what I participated in. I created a fantasy in my mind that convinced me this was what I needed in order to mask the pain in my heart.

There a few different manifestations of pain we may see. Some pain causes us to get a 'tough skin' while others may experience extreme sensitivity to everything and anything which causes them to appear soft or weak. Some will become numb to all pain. There are those who have suffered so much in their lives they have trained themselves to no longer feel the effects of pain. This can be the most dangerous as the person is so hardened it is difficult for them to allow freedom in. Hardness of heart can be a learned behavior as well. It is also a defense mechanism. Do any of these sound familiar?

- Be strong
- Be tough
- Keep the family secret private
- Hide it
- Be responsible
- Be a man

- Get over it
- Grow up
- Don't be a punk

All of these sayings or phrases are things we may say to one another but yet are we realizing that with each phrase the receiver's heart is hardening? Every time the words are launched towards another that person is learning to stuff their pain deeper and deeper inside themselves instead of releasing it completely.

Pain extended over long periods of time will eventually lead to a breakdown that cannot be hidden. You may be able to get by for some time with the results of pain hidden behind a mask you wear in public, but it will not last forever. The buildup will eventually make you blow. Some may believe moving on means you are free from the pain. In all reality, the pain is still present, it is just dormant. We were not designed to carry all of these types of things. We were designed to give it all over to Jesus. The bible tells us in 1 Peter 5:7 "Give all your worries and cares to God, for He cares about what happens to you". Pain should drive us closer to the Lord and drive us deeper into His heart. The bible says in Psalm 147:3 "He heals the brokenhearted, binding up their wounds." The bible also tells us that there is hope beyond the pain and suffering we see in front of us. In 2 Corinthians 4:16-18 it says "That is why we never give up. Though our bodies are dying, our spirits are being renewed every day. For our present troubles are quite small and won't last very long. Yet they produce for us an immeasurable great glory that will last forever. So we don't look at the trouble we can see right now; rather, we look forward to what we have not yet seen. For the troubles we see will soon be over, but the joys to come will last forever."

Prayer: Father, I release every ounce of pain I have experienced, carried, and held onto. I know you want me to cast all my cares and burdens upon you. I no longer want to hang onto the pain I have felt in the past nor the pain I have experienced recently. I desire to be free from the effects of pain in my life. I need your help to forgive those who have caused me pain and even the pain I have self-inflicted. Deliver me Lord from any and all addictive behaviors I have allowed as I have tried to mask what I didn't want to see, hear, or feel. Forgive me for running to those things instead of running straight to you. I desperately need you to help me become free. I want to forgive. I want to love. I want wholeness. I invite your healing power into my life now. I invite your wholeness into my life now. Break the chains of bondage which have kept me entangled in the cycle and web of pain now. In the name of Jesus, I decree and declare that I am healed! I speak to the deepest parts of me and command you to be healed and receiving healing oil from heaven. I will no longer walk with the mindset or behaviors of the effects of pain. Holy Spirit teach me how to let it all go. I am thankful to you Jesus. I am grateful for your power to set me free from it all. I am blessed for the process of freedom from pain. You are so good. You are faithful and loving and I love you. Thank you Jesus.

Heart Check Up

♡ What areas of your life are you holding on to pain?

♡ What caused this pain to take a hold of your heart?

♡ Who do you need to forgive and from what?

♡ Do you have addictive behaviors that stem from pain? If so, what are they and what action steps are you going to take to discontinue operating in those behaviors?

5 SUICIDE

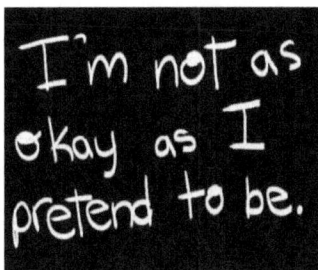

There were so many moments in life where I could be surrounded by tons of people and yet still feel so alone. Thoughts would plague my mind constantly. No one loved me. No one fought for me. No one desired me just for me and not for what I would or could do for them. If I disappeared would anyone notice? Would they even care if they did notice? As I mentioned before I struggled for a long time not really identifying with who I was in Christ. My worth and value was in man's opinion of me.

I battled with that silent, hidden depression. The kind that smiles and laughs and looks like everything is just swell. Inside I was locked in a cage screaming for someone to help me get out. I probably could have won an Oscar for my performances. My struggle became so serious within myself that I contemplated how to take my life on several occasions. I would sit and plan in my mind how I could just end the internal turmoil and be free from it all. Or perhaps hurt myself just enough to make people care about me. Would anyone come visit me? Would anyone care I was a mess? My self-worth was so low I believe it could have become one with the core of the earth. My children (at the time I had two sons) kept me. My love for them superseded my feelings and they literally kept me alive.

Jesus had to come crashing in to rescue me. He had to come in like a violent storm and show me "I paid for you! You are worth it! I want you! I choose you! I need you! Don't give up! Don't give up!" His beckoning of me sent me deep into the worship of Him. It was all I had. In my worship, in my raw prayers before Him, healing began.

When I made the choice to be transparent before God was the very moment I felt Him say "Now, I can begin. I've been waiting for you. Beautiful one, I've been waiting."

Worship Arts Ministers I know there are more of you out there who were or are like I was. There is hope. Don't give in to the lies the enemy will try to plague you with. You can't lead well or be effective in your call or ministry when you are experiencing these things. You are not alone. Don't hide. Don't hide anymore. He wants you to be free! Your personal worship will change completely and those you lead in corporate worship-through whatever art form you use to express yourself-will be drawn deeper, wider, and higher in the very heart of God.

When I bore it all before the Lord in my tiny closet, this song began to play on my YouTube. He sang to me beloved reader. He sang to me. He wants to sing to you too. Will you let Him?

Come out of hiding
You're safe here with Me
There's no need to cover
What I already see
You've got your reasons
But I hold your peace
You've been on lock-down
And I hold the key

'Cause I loved you before you knew it was love
And I saw it all, still I chose the cross
And you were the one that I was thinking of
When I rose from the grave
Now rid of the shackles, My victory's yours
I tore the veil for you to come close
There's no reason to stand at a distance anymore
You're not far from home

And now I'll be your lighthouse
When you're lost at sea
And I will illuminate
Everything
No need to be frightened by intimacy
No, just throw off your fear
And come running to Me

'Cause I loved you before you knew it was love
And I saw it all, still I chose the cross
And you were the one that I was thinking of
When I rose from the grave
Now rid of the shackles, My victory's yours
I tore the veil for you to come close
There's no reason to stand at a distance anymore
You're not far from home
You're not far from home
Keep on coming

And oh, as you run
What hindered love
Will only become
Part of the story
And oh, as you run
What hindered love
Will only become
Part of the story
And oh, as you run
What hindered love
Will only become
Part of the story
And oh as you run
What hindered love
Will only become
Part of the story

Baby, you're almost home now
Please don't quit now
You're almost home to me, yeah
Baby, you're almost home now
Please don't quit now
You're almost home to me, yes you are
Now baby, you're almost home now
Please don't quit now
You're almost home to me

Songwriters: Steffany Gretzinger
Out of Hiding lyrics © Bethel Music Dba Bethel Music Publishing

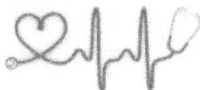

Heart Check Up

Have you ever felt such hopelessness you wanted to take your life? If yes, write out every feeling or emotion you have felt or are feeling, THEN, write the opposite and begin to declare life over yourself. Ugly-beautiful, Unwanted-loved, Desperate-fully satisfied, Broken-Wholeness. For example, I've felt lost and alone but the bible says Jesus will never leave me or forsake me. The bible also says he places the brokenhearted in families.

Do you know someone else who may have tried to take their life or considered it? What can you do to encourage them and offer them hope through the Word of God?

Have you shared with someone you can trust about your

thoughts and feelings or does pride keep you silent? Don't stay silent-punch pride in the face and say something. Perhaps you haven't considered taking your life BUT you have felt hopeless, desperate, or trapped inside yourself. Share with someone, have a repentant heart, and accept forgiveness and freedom as you move forward. So, what is your plan? Pick up the phone, call someone, schedule a date and start releasing what has been dormant or hidden.

Who am I calling/reaching out to?

_____

When are we connecting?

_____

What would I like to share and why?

_____

What do I need freedom and healing from?

_____

6 SUBMISSION

Submission is not a bad word. Many of us can admit that in hearing this word our immediate reaction may not be "oh yes I just love me some submission!" To the contrary our first and even long term reaction may be somewhat negative. Submission in churches and ministries and also in the secular world is a term that is not embraced as positive. Why is this? What is it about this word which causes angst among people? The term or preconceived act of submission has been used inappropriately to control and manipulate instead of being an area of great blessing and honor.

The word submission is a noun and means: the action or fact of accepting or yielding to a superior or to the will or author of another person.

> *Submission is not a bad word.*

I had a hard time learning what true submission really was for many years until the Lord in His loving and gracious manner began to show me. It is not that he didn't want to show me before, but I wasn't in any way, shape, or form looking for an answer about what submission should actually be.

Remember when I shared how my father taught me to be so independent yet controlled my mother under the pretense of 'wives submit to your husbands…"? I had a very warped understanding and viewpoint on submission. I struggled for many years in my marriage during the early stages for various reasons but one major area was submission. I didn't want to be told what to do, how to do it or when to do it. I could handle or take care of things on my own and truly believed I was consistently right. After all it was ingrained in my head. "Be the best! Depend on no one! You take charge!"

The examples I saw in church growing up weren't necessarily healthy at all. I witnessed submission teachings, demonstration, and woman's' lives under so-called submission from God who were controlled, abused, manipulated, and treated so harshly by their spouses I couldn't understand how this could really even be biblical.

Holy Spirit taught in later years what this is supposed to look like. He brought Apostle Elizabeth Hairston-McBurrows into my life and He worked through her to teach me so much. She emulates the character of Christ in everything she does and she patiently and loving worked on teaching me just what I needed to receive from the Lord. She mothered me both in the natural sense and also spiritually. She has labored in prayer with me and for me and taught me so much. As my spiritual mother, she took her position seriously. She never-to this day-has been cruel, mean, controlling, or hard towards me. Don't get me wrong my mama will correct and rebuke when necessary but you walk away from time spent with her or conversations had with her feeling uplifted and encouraged even when you are receiving correction. She allowed me to walk alongside her on many occasions in both corporate and private settings. As I walked with her I learned. As I observed her I learned.

One of the very first things I learned from Apostle was submission. She taught me how to submit and surrender my heart completely to the Lord and how to have the heart of a servant. She sat with me in her living room in Albuquerque, NM and poured into me for hours. I learned from what she spoke and even more from the unspoken.

Her life and character spoke for her. She taught me the beauty of submission to Christ first and then to those in authority over us. I had many a humbling moments in her presence, but the Lord worked through those moments to teach me.

One of the parts of the definition of submission you may notice is 'yield'. It has actually become one of my favorite words. Yielding is a personal choice. Yielding is not pure when it is forced upon a person. Pure, intentional yielding is a place in the Lord which is so beautiful for so many reasons, but one big one is that in the place of yieldedness before Him in His presence is where He can and does so easily come right in and fill you up with all of Himself. In that place you lessen and He can increase. In that place He heals, restores, transforms, empower, refreshes, and pours out His love. All things come together with Him in this place perfectly. We weren't created to be self sufficient. We were created for relationship with Jesus. In our relationship with Him there are boundaries He established for our safety, covering, and protection. We yield to His will, His way, and His plan and in turn we receive blessing, covering, protection, and favor. There is no control in His presence. There is no manipulation in His presence. His presence is pure and untainted with the distortion of this worlds thinking.

If you aren't in true full submission to the Lord you won't really know how to emulate this in other areas of your life.

When you cannot embrace submission as a gift from God, you will find it very difficult to submit to your spouse, your boss, your pastors and leaders. If you aren't in true full submission to the Lord you won't really know how to emulate this in other areas of your life. I have experienced for myself and seen this struggle in areas of ministries and churches over the years. You can't half submit. You can't submit to the leaders you like but half step or flat out refuse to submit to those you don't care for. Perhaps a leader hasn't treated you kindly or fairly and you feel you are justified. Guess what? You are wrong. You are called to submit (not be controlled by) your leaders regardless of your feelings towards them. When you follow the beautiful biblical design of submission you truly align yourself to be a conduit of the blessings of the Lord.

5 Steps to Walk in Healthy Biblical Submission to Authority

These steps are guides to help you cultivate and maintain healthy relationships with your leaders and yourself as a follower. Each of these steps is also quite valuable in marriage relationships as the husband is the head (leader) and the wife is the one who follows (support).

1. Understand no leader is perfect. (None of us are!) Leaders are going to make mistakes. I like what one minister says: leaders are "deficient by design." They are not meant to take the place of God in our life. They're going to need help, and need our prayers. God tells us to pray for all those in position of authority so we can live peaceful lives (1 Timothy 2:2). It's not just a suggestion. When we disagree with our leader, the first thing we should do pray for them (not talk about them) – and don't stop!

2. Let's find out…Who's the boss? We are all accountable to someone. As helpers and followers, you and I are stewards of someone else's vision. God has a divine order to things, and when He wants something done, He raises up a leader. He also raises up people to help the leader. Be sure you know which one is which, and then act accordingly. We are God's Army, there's a rank and file, and a way to do things (Ephesians 4, 1 Cor. 12:18, Hebrews 13:17). Many times you would not do things the same way your leader would, but different methods can accomplish the same goals, and someone has to lead.

3. There's a big picture and vision and if you're not the leader, you don't always see it. There's a lot you don't know – and may never know. Depending on your role (how closely you work with leader), you are there to support them in accomplishing the organization's purpose, either up close or at a distance. Take seriously the power and responsibility of "followership." Your ideas might be good ideas, but they might not be God ideas in the current scheme of things. You'll be happiest when you fit in with and contribute to the vision that's in place. We are all most effective for the kingdom when we pray what Jesus prayed in Luke 22:42 – "not my will, Lord, but yours be done."

4. Understand your position. If you're part of the decision-making process, or your opinion is sought, give it. (Also remember that it's the leader's communication style that determines the dialogue, not yours. And remember if you're giving your opinion, timing is everything). Understand that having the leader's ear comes from relationship, and you're going to have to prove yourself first. Are you someone the leader wants to hear from? If not, then keep quiet – be faithful, put your hand to the plow, be a help, and pray. Develop trustworthiness. That takes time.

5. Trust God. Hopefully you're serving the Lord, not serving a leader (Colossians 3:17). It's not our place to correct our leader; God put them in position, so if we have issues, we can go to God about it, and trust HIM. If there are serious problems, perhaps we can address an accountability person – but don't spread your opinion around or look for people to agree with you. Don't sow discord (Prov. 13:3, 6:12-19). Instead, pray and trust God. Spend the time and expect the answer. Ask yourself, "Is this just me? Or is it a real problem?" Give it time before talking with anyone else about it.

When you disagree with your leader, remember there is always One higher than they – it's God your Father. He knows how to work all things together for good (Romans 8:28). You can trust Him. Bring all your cares to Him, serve Him with all your heart, stay in the Word, keep your joy, and do everything in love (1 Corinthians 16:14).

15 Rewards for Submission

Reward 1: Things will be well with you.
The bible says in Ephesians 6:2-3 "Honor thy father and mother; which is the first commandment with promise; that it may be well with you".

Reward 2: You will have a long life.
The bible says in Ephesians 6:1-3 "Children, obey your parents in the Lord, for this is right. "Honor your father and mother"—which is the first commandment with a promise- "so that it may go well with you and that you may enjoy long life on the earth."

Reward 3: You will bring delight to the Lord.
The bible says in Colossians 3:20 "Children, obey your parents in all things: for this is well pleasing to the Lord".

Reward 4: You will avoid fear of condemnation.
The bible says in Romans 13:3-4 "For rulers hold no terror for those who do right, but for those who do wrong. Do you want to be free from fear of the one in authority? Then do what is right and you will be commended. For the one in authority is God's servant for your good. But if you do wrong, be afraid, for rulers do not bear the sword for no reason. They are God's servants, agents of wrath to bring punishment on the wrongdoer"

Reward 5: You will maintain a good conscience.
The bible says in Romans 13:5 "Therefore, it is necessary to submit to the authorities, not only because of possible punishment but also as a matter of conscience."

Reward 6: You will bring joy to your authorities.
The bible says in Hebrews 13:17 "Have confidence in your leaders and submit to their authority, because they keep watch over you as those who must give an account. Do this so that their work will be a joy, not a burden, for that would be of no benefit to you."

Reward 7: You will receive God's reward.

The bible says in Colossians 3:18-24 "Wives, submit yourselves to your husbands, as is fitting in the Lord. Husbands, love your wives and do not be harsh with them. Children, obey your parents in everything, for this pleases the Lord. Fathers, do not embitter your children, or they will become discouraged. Slaves, obey your earthly masters in everything; and do it, not only when their eye is on you and to curry their favor, but with sincerity of heart and reverence for the Lord. Whatever you do, work at it with all your heart, as working for the Lord, not for human masters, since you know that you will receive an inheritance from the Lord as a reward. It is the Lord Christ you are serving."

Reward 8: You will avoid blaspheming God and His Word through rebellion.
The bible says in 1 Timothy 6:1 "All who are under the yoke of slavery should consider their masters worthy of full respect, so that God's name and our teaching may not be slandered."

Reward 9: You will be given clear direction.
The bible says Proverbs 6:20-22 "My son, obey your father's commands, and don't neglect your mother's instruction. Keep their words always in your heart. Tie them around your neck. When you walk, their counsel will lead you. When you sleep, they will protect you. When you wake up, they will advise you."

Reward 10: You will be protected from evil people.
The bible says in Proverbs 6:23-24 "For their command is a lamp and their instruction a light; their corrective discipline is the way to life. It will keep you from the immoral woman, from the smooth tongue of a promiscuous woman."

Reward 11: You will gain discernment.
The bible says in Proverbs 15:5 "Only a fool despises a parent's discipline; whoever learns from correction is wise."

Reward 12: You will receive praise from your authorities.
The bible says in 1 Peter 2:13-14 "For the Lord's sake, submit to all human authority—whether the king as head of state, or the officials he has appointed. For the king has sent them to punish those who do wrong and to honor those who do right."

Reward 13: You will honor those whom God has placed in authority over you.
The bible says in 1 Thessalonians 5:12-13 "Dear brothers and sisters, honor those who are your leaders in the Lord's work. They work hard among you and give you spiritual guidance.[13] Show them great respect and wholehearted love because of their work. And live peacefully with each other."

Reward 14: You will escape the destruction of pride.
The bible says in 1 Timothy 6:2-4 "If the masters are believers, that is no excuse for being disrespectful. Those slaves should work all the harder because their efforts are helping other believers who are well loved. Teach these things, Timothy, and encourage everyone to obey them. Some people may contradict our teaching, but these are the wholesome teachings of the Lord Jesus Christ. These teachings promote a godly life. Anyone who teaches something different is arrogant and lacks understanding. Such a person has an unhealthy desire to quibble over the meaning of words. This stirs up arguments

Reward 15: You will receive the grace God gives to the humble.
The bible says in 1 Peter 5:5-7 "In the same way, you who are younger must accept the authority of the elders. And all of you, dress yourselves in humility as you relate to one another, for "God opposes the proud but gives grace to the humble." So humble yourselves under the mighty power of God, and at the right time he will lift you up in honor. Give all your worries and cares to God, for he cares about you."

When you don't submit to your leaders, pastors, boss or spouse you are basically telling God His way is flawed. You are letting Him know you have a better idea and understanding of how things should go. Oh that's right Creator of the Universe, my way is better. Think again my friend.

I struggled with this for years. I would tell myself I submit to God because I can trust Him. I can submit to what He says but all these other people-no way Jose. What I didn't truly realize was I wasn't submitting to God at all. If I had been I would also be submitting myself to those in authority over me and I wasn't. You either do or you don't. Half way means you don't.

Obedience goes hand in hand with submission. Obey immediately and without questions. Submit yourself fully to the Lord and trust Him that those He has called and placed in authority over you are part of His overall plan for your life. When you struggle with any of the issues or ideals we discussed, give it over to Him in prayer and avoid dissension, disunity, or discord. Run to the throne of the Master instead of the phone to gossip or slander.

Submission is good. It's perfectly designed by God for our good and to bless us.

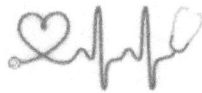

Heart Check Up

Do you struggle with submission? If so, in what areas of your life?

Are there areas in your life that you are able to submit with more ease than others? Reflect and ask yourself 'why?'.

♡ Are you sincerely praying for your spouse (if you have one), your pastors, leaders, those in authority over you? Answer honestly and if you are not, what are you going to do differently?

_____

_____

_____

_____

_____

_____

_____

_____

_____

_____

_____

_____

_____

_____

_____

_____

_____

_____

Prayer: Father God, I acknowledge who you are and that you are seated on the throne in Heaven. Jesus I acknowledge and affirm you are seated at our Father's right hand in heaven continuously interceding for me. Holy Spirit I acknowledge and affirm you are here present with me on the earth. I submit myself to you. I submit my cares, wants, thoughts, and desires to you. I yield my own opinions and ways to the foot of the cross. I repent for the areas in my heart and life where I have not allowed the spirit of submission to fully operate. Destroy pride in my life. Destroy arrogance in my life. Spirit of the living God dismantle and destroy divisiveness in my life. I command, by the finger of God, all resistance to submission and humbly to be cast out of my life NOW. I decree and declare I have a submissive heart and mind. I walk in obedience to Christ and all of His ways. I am not divisive. I do not create discord. I do not resist correction. I do not sow deceit. I do not publicly praise yet privately tear down my leaders. I shut down gossip and slander immediately and do not partner with this manner of evil when it comes my way. I pray at all times for all things and submit my cares and concerns to the Lord. I yield to the movement of the Holy Spirit in my life and receive and embrace His loving correction because I know it is for my good. I will walk in the fruits of the spirit and shine forth the light of Christ in my life in order for man to see the light of truth and in turn be drawn into the Kingdom of God. I will obey my spouse as directed by the Word of God. I will obey those in authority over me as directed by the Word of God. I will uplift and honor those in authority over me. In turn, I will be rewarded by the Lord for my heart of obedience and faithfulness to His Word. My name will be associated with honor, integrity, peace, forgiveness, unity, and most importantly LOVE. Seal this all in my heart Jesus. I yield to you fully and completely on this day. Have your way in my life.

7 UNFORGIVENESS

I have heard this saying several times over the course of my life, but honestly it didn't truly sink in for me personally until I allowed God to expose Unforgiveness in my own heart. The saying is this: Unforgiveness is like drinking a bottle of poison and expecting the other person to get sick. That statement could not be more true beloved reader. When we choose (because it IS a choice) to hang on to Unforgiveness we are poisoning ourselves and yet the other person, persons, or organizations are just fine going about their business as usual. We on the other hand allow ourselves to become infected with a cancer which metastasizes-or grows and spreads-throughout our mind, body, soul and spirit. What we then have allowed is for the cancer of unforgivenss to make a banqueting table for hurt, pain, offense, bitterness and anger to feast upon. We have spent a few chapters together talking about these very things, yet that ALL stems from some form of unforgiveness.

> Unforgiveness is a major blockage for God to move or respond in your life.

Dearest worshipper, unforgivenss is a major blockage for God to move or respond in your life. If you are supposed to be the conduit in which he flows through in order to teach others, draw others to Him, and lead others into His very presence, you cannot do this effectively if you allow Unforgiveness to take residence in your heart.

The bible says in Ephesians 4:46-47 "And don't sin by letting anger control you. Don't let the sun go down while you are still angry, for anger gives a foothold to the devil".

Don't hold on to things. Resolve it quickly and move forward.

The bible says in Matthew 5:23-24 "So if you are presenting a sacrifice at the altar in the Temple and you suddenly remember that someone has something against you, leave your sacrifice there at the altar. Go and be reconciled to that person. Then come and offer your sacrifice to God."

When you are going before the Lord in worship corporately, take the time to make sure your heart is clean and if it isn't take care of what is in your heart immediately. It is important to the Lord that you do this BEFORE you come to offer Him anything. Handle your business and remove any hindrances which may be present so when you stand before the Lord you can do so with a clear conscience.

The bible says Matthew 18:21-22 "Then Peter came to him and asked, Lord, how often should I forgive someone who sins against me? Seven times? No, not seven times, Jesus replied, but seventy times seven."

Be forgiving. It truly is that simple. Extend the same grace and mercy the Lord continually extends towards you on a daily basis to those who surround you in life. Forgive over and over and over again. We will err and falter here on earth. People will need us to forgive them just as we need to have them forgive us-continually.

> *Be forgiving. It truly is that simple.*

The bible says in Mark 11:25 "But when you are praying, first forgive anyone you are holding a grudge against, so that your Father in heaven will forgive your sins, too."

Before the Father will attune His ears to us and forgive us as we dialogue with Him in prayer, He is giving us clear instructions that in order for him to forgive us and hear us in our prayers, it is necessary for us to release grudges we have against other people.

At some point in our lives, we have all received this type of teaching and instruction on unforgiveness, however without application it means absolutely nothing. Don't stay bigheaded or fat with lots of knowledge yet you are not applying any of it to your own life.

I held unforgiveness in my heart for many years. Some I was fully aware of and chose to hang onto it. I really felt I had the right to not forgive. After all, I was hurt abused, taken advantage of, mistreated, discarded, and felt unloved by so many. I deserved to not forgive. Wow! I was so lost.

Christ died because He loved me and eradicated my filth. He died knowing how much I would fail Him over and over yet He forgave it all out of pure love for me. No strings attached. He chose to love me through every step.

In my blindness toward my unforgiveness I could not see that I was hurting myself more and more each day I held onto it, nor did I realize how it affected those around me because of the manifestations or results in my day to day behaviors. I was often bothered with people, short tempered, had no patience or tolerance for anything which directly affected my selfish nature I had adopted, and I was just not a nice person. Period.

I went through various stages of healing, repentance, and deliverance over the year and Jesus literally had to tear down fortresses-not just walls-but fortresses I had built around my heart to protect myself. I couldn't be free otherwise. It was similar to plaque build up around the arteries of the heart. It starts small and seemingly harmless or unnoticed, but it will kill you slowly and silently if it goes undetected. The build up goes undetected until you begin to experience pressure or tightness in your chest, shortness of breath, or worse have a heart attack. In the background for days, moths, and years this plaque has been building up more and more until proper blood flow-our life source-cannot function properly and life comes to an alarming halt.

Our spiritual life is very reflective of what we see in the natural effects of this plaque build up. Offense, bitterness, hurt/pain, and resentment are all forms of things which can clog our spiritual arteries so to speak.

The flow and ease in which the blood can flow becomes hindered because of the plaque build up. Soon we see the flow become completely blocked and death knocks on the door. Spiritual death is imminent if intervention and proper treatment is not administered immediately. Part of that treatment will require your 'Yes' to God. It will require you yielding and saying "Here I am lord, I surrender. I release all unforgiveness and I invite you in as my Master Surgeon to correct all I have allowed and to eradicate the build up I have invited into my life. Clean it up God. Clean it out. I surrender every aspect." This, dear one, will cause you to reflect and even forgive yourself, yes, yourself. We can oftentimes not even realize how much unforgiveness we hold towards ourselves. If we don't recognize and surrender this as well, we will constantly be captive in the prison cell of unforgivenss towards ourselves. I experienced this bondage myself and had no idea I was captive. It took one mentor I had in my life at the time when I was struggling with understand why I couldn't see personal breakthrough in areas of my life and was having repeated emotions, cycles, and behaviors. I just couldn't figure out why. One day she looked me straight in the eyes and she said "Have you forgive yourself?" I was stunned. My response to her was "Pffftt…shoot girl what do you mean? I'm good. All is well. I just need you to tell me what I am not seeing." Again, she said "Have you forgive yourself?" Immediately God began to show me like a movie reel in front of my eyes all the places of unforgiveness I had towards myself. I had to forgive myself for resentment toward my father. I had to forgive myself for hatred I allowed to grow in my heart towards those who hurt me. I had to forgive myself for what I thought was not being a good enough mother. I had to forgive myself for not protecting my children enough from enduring my mistakes. I had to forgive myself for shaming myself countless times with my body and not saying "No! I am worth more than this." I had to forgive myself because I truly was not perfect. I had to forgive myself for not being forgiving. I saw it all and it is so much more than even this.

I broke immediately and just screamed and cried. I could feel the Lord tearing down, brick by brick, the lies the enemy convinced me were truth over the years. Each brick gave me a sense of deeper healing and more freedom until I was completely free 100 percent. It is hard to explain in mere words, but I literally felt cages of death, despair, and destruction fall ooff of the caverns of my heart. Immediately they unlocked and crashed to the ground. I was experiencing deliverance in those moments and Jesus was setting me free.

Up to the point in my journey with Jesus, I was still yielding to Him and purposing to obey Him, but the flow of His power and anointing was hindered because of my own personal unforgiveness. Did I teach? Yes. Did I minister? Yes. Did I see God move? Yes. BUT when I truly became completely free, I experienced His love and compassion for the lost in an exponential manner and His power and anointing on my life sky rocketed. He blew my mind over and over again. I was also able to minister to broken hearts that were scarred by unforgiveness and see them healed and set free. The grace and anointing on my life had increased so I could minister healing and deliverance to each of them from a place of having been delivered already myself.

This goes for many areas of life and in ministry, but for the sake of focus in this chapter we will hone in on hearts of unforgiveness. Once you have been delivered dear one, you will have an increase in discernment to spot this stronghold in others. It is not your job to call out in judgement what you recognize, but it is your responsibility to cover and approach, under the Lord's direction, the person with genuine love and compassion. Then with your authority given to you through Christ Jesus, call the spirit of unforgiveness out and subject it to the cross. Command the forgiving power of the blood of Jesus to bathe over them and for the love and peace of God to overwhelm them. It has happened to me many times. There have even been instances when Holy Spirit will prompt me to go to a person who has stuff in their heart towards me personally or perhaps someone close to me. They have never told me or displayed it but Holy Spirit allows me to see it. As I have been delivered from it, addressing it head on comes with ease. I just allow Holy Spirit to flood them with love as I typically just embrace the person with very few-if any-words. Holy Spirit does the work and then opens the way for forgiveness to flow. It is just so beautiful to see him move.

Forgiveness is a daily-moment by moment, hour by hour process. Remain humble and do not ever think so highly of yourself in which you deceive yourself into thinking you have arrived. Stay humble before God. Stay in a position of worship. It is in this place of intimate exchange where Christ will continue to care for your heart as you allow Him to romance you and you romance Him.

As worship arts ministers, it is our mandate to walk continuously in a lifestyle of worship. Part of that is making sure your heart is pure before God and unforgiveness is far from you. You cannot effectively minister or lead others when your own personal flow is blocked by spiritual plaque. You want clear vessels for Him to flow through. No one is perfect but Jesus; however, as we follow Him and become more like Him every day, we should see a decrease in how often we have to experience deliverance from unforgiveness. Be quick to obey Him. Be quick to forgive and have a yielded repentant heart before Him.

God's forgiveness is not based on what we do or do not do. Allow me to be clear. It is a free gift given because of His love for us. Forgiveness is founded completely n God and by Jesus blood shed on the cross. When we can sit back and truly grasp the greatness of God's gift to us, we will pass the gift along with joy.

We have been given grace and should give grace to others in return. The bible tells a parable in Matthew 18:21-35 which says "Then Peter came to him and asked, "Lord, how often should I forgive someone who sins against me? Seven times?" "No, not seven times," Jesus replied, "but seventy times seven! "Therefore, the Kingdom of Heaven can be compared to a king who decided to bring his accounts up to date with servants who had borrowed money from him. In the process, one of his debtors was brought in who owed him millions of dollars.He couldn't pay, so his master ordered that he be sold—along with his wife, his children, and everything he owned—to pay the debt. "But the man fell down before his master and begged him,

'Please, be patient with me, and I will pay it all.' Then his master was filled with pity for him, and he released him and forgave his debt. "But when the man left the king, he went to a fellow servant who owed him a few thousand dollars. He grabbed him by the throat and demanded instant payment." His fellow servant fell down before him and begged for a little more time. 'Be patient with me, and I will pay it,' he pleaded. But his creditor wouldn't wait. He had the man arrested and put in prison until the debt could be paid in full. "When some of the other servants saw this, they were very upset. They went to the king and told him everything that had happened. Then the king called in the man he had forgiven and said, 'You evil servant! I forgave you that tremendous debt because you pleaded with me. Shouldn't you have mercy on your fellow servant, just as I had mercy on you?' Then the angry king sent the man to prison to be tortured until he had paid his entire debt." "That's what my heavenly Father will do to you if you refuse to forgive your brothers and sisters from your heart."

> *Unforgiveness robs us of the full life God has intended for us.*

In this parable we are appalled at the servant who would not forgive a minor debt after having been forgiven his unpaid debt. But when we are unforgiving towards others and ourselves, we are acting just like the servant in the parable.

Unforgiveness robs us of the full life God has intended for us. The Zoe, or abundant life. Rather than proclaiming justice, love and joy, our tendency and habit to hold onto unforgiveness begins to fester bitterness. It is comparable to a plaque build up in our arteries. The bible says in Hebrews 12:14-15 "Work at living in peace with everyone, and work at living a holy life, for those who are not holy will not see the Lord. Look after each other so that none of you fails to receive the grace of God. Watch out that no poisonous root of bitterness grows up to trouble you, corrupting many." Also in 2 Corinthians 2:5-11 we read "I am not overstating it when I say that the man who caused all the trouble hurt all of you more than he hurt me. Most of you opposed him, and that was punishment enough. Now, however, it is time to forgive and comfort him. Otherwise he may be overcome by discouragement. So I urge you now to reaffirm your love for him. I wrote to you as I did to test you and see if you would fully comply with my instructions. When you forgive this man, I forgive him, too. And when I forgive whatever needs to be forgiven, I do so with Christ's authority for your benefit, so that Satan will not outsmart us. For we are familiar with his evil schemes." It is a warning that unforgiveness can be an open door for satan to attempt to derail us.

You may ask yourself "How about those who have truly hurt us or brought trauma in our lives. I forgive, but what about what THEY did? Leave it to God. Forgive and be free!

We should know that those who have sinned against us-who we don't want to forgive-are held accountable by God. The bible says in Romans 12:19 "Dear friends, never take revenge. Leave that to the righteous anger of God. For the Scriptures say, "I will take revenge; I will pay them back," says the LORD."

We also read in the bible in Hebrews 10:30 "For we know the one who said, "I will take revenge. I will pay them back." He also said, "The LORD will judge his own people."

It is vitally important to understand and recognize that to forgive is not to downplay a wrongdoing or necessarily to reconcile. When we make a choice to forgive, we release a person from indebtedness to us. We honestly relinquish or surrender our right to seek personal revenge. We choose to admit and say we will not hold their wrongdoing against them. However, we do not necessarily allow the person back into our trust or even fully release them from natural consequences of sin. The bible says in Romans 6:23 "The wages of sin is death." God's forgiveness relieves us and them from eternal death. It does not always simply prevent death-like consequences such as broken relationships, separations, or penalties brought on by the law. Forgiveness doesn't mean we just act as if no wrong ha been done, but it does mean we can recognize the amazing grace that has been given to us so we have no right to hold someone else's wrongdoing over their head.

The bible tells us over and over to forgive each other. How many times have you sinned in your life? How about this year? This month? This day? Just in the last few moments? Okay, so Christ forgave and forgives continually as should we.

> *When we disobey God we are obeying satan. Where do you want your obedience to be associated with?*

The bible says in Ephesians 4:32 "Instead, be kind to each other, tenderhearted, forgiving one another, just as God through Christ has forgiven you."

We have been given so much in the way of forgiveness, and much is expected from us in response. Luke 12:48 says "But someone who does not know, and then does something wrong, will be punished only lightly.

When someone has been given much, much will be required in return; and when someone has been entrusted with much, even more will be required." Although forgiveness is often so hard to do, to have an unforgiving heart is to disobey God and devalue the greatness of His gift to us.

When we disobey God we are obeying satan. Where do you want your obedience to be associated with?

"The ultimate proof of total forgiveness takes place when we sincerely petition the Father to let those who have hurt us off the hook-even if they have hurt not only us, but those close to us." -
R.T. Kendall

"We must develop and maintain the capacity to forgive. He who is devoid of the power to forgive is devoid of the power of love. There is some good in the worst of us and some evil in the best of us. When we discover this, we are less prone to hate." -
Martin Luther King Jr.

"It is one of the greatest gifts you can give yourself, to forgive. Forgive everybody."

Maya Angelou

"The weak can never forgive. Forgiveness is the attribute of the strong."
–Mahatma Gandhi

"When a deep injury is done to us, we never heal until we forgive." – Nelson Mandela

"Blame keeps wounds open. Only forgiveness heals."
–Thomas S. Manson

"Forgiveness is a choice, but it is not an option"
–Joel Osteen

"I forgive myself and I set myself free"
–Louise Hay

"If we really want to love we must learn how to forgive."
–Mother Theresa

"To be a Christian means to forgive the inexcusable because God has forgiven the inexcusable in you."
–C.S. Lewis

"Forgiveness is not a feeling; it is a choice to show mercy, not to hold the offense up against the offender. Forgiveness is a [true] expression of love."
–Gary Chapman

"Forgiveness is the fragrance that the violet sheds on the heel that has crushed it."
-Mark Twain

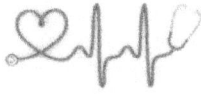

Heart Check Up

Who do you need to forgive and why?

_____

_____

_____

_____

What do you need to forgive about yourself?

_____

_____

_____

_____

Release it all to the Lord.

Prayer: Father, in the name of Jesus I completely yield and relinquish to you Unforgiveness I have in my heart towards _____. I refuse to hold onto it any longer. I give you permission to rush into the caverns of my heart and clear out the debris of Unforgiveness. I want to be free. I want to be whole. Beautiful Jesus wash me. Refresh. Renew. Revive. Restore Lord. Your word tells me whom the son sets free is free indeed. Your word also tells me where the spirit of the Lord is there is freedom. So I invite your spirit Lord to breathe a fresh wind over me and resurrect what was stamped with death.

I have life and have it abundantly in all areas of my life. I decree and I declare I am free from Unforgiveness. I receive your love and I receive your forgiveness.

8 BETRAYAL

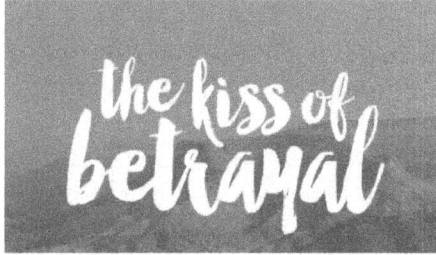
the kiss of betrayal

Everyone needs a Judas in their life. Say what? Yes, it is true. A Judas will help to propel you towards your destiny. See, the enemy would absolutely love for a Judas to choke the life out of your destiny and purpose; he would love to see you succumb to the sting of betrayal and curse God, he would also love to see divisions, disunity, and discord sown among God's kids. He thrives off of that. However, embrace the Judas experience and allow it to be used to glorify God. When you experience the depths of pain betrayal can cause the best place to run is into the arms of Jesus. It is in that perfect place of love and compassion where Jesus can and will take what the enemy planned and intended for evil and harm and turn that entire situation out for good.

The word betrayal is a verb or an action word which tells us it is not a passive word but has very specific intention and movement. Betrayal defined is to deliver or to expose to an enemy by treachery or disloyalty. It also means to be unfaithful in guarding, maintaining or fulfilling a trust. Betrayal means to disappoint the hopes or expectations of; be disloyal to. It can mean to reveal or disclose in violation of confidence. Betrayal can mean to deceive, misguide or corrupts. Lastly, betrayal can be defined as to seduce and then desert. (Dictionary.com)

I have been betrayed countless times in my life. I have experienced it in personal relationships, in my marriage, in corporate and ministerial settings, in friendships, in church, outside of church, in my own home and in ministry. Betrayal only hurts when it is done by those closest to you. Similar to offense, it is not as traumatic when it is done by someone from a distance. The sting of betrayal burns because the person was so close. I have had people who were very close to me smile in my face and show forth supposed trust, love and loyalty only to eventually find out they had not been genuine all along. I have seen people bless me to my face yet curse me behind my back. I have had those who waved palm branches figuratively one week and the next were screaming "Crucify her!" I am in no way comparing myself to Jesus, but simply using it as an example. I have had 'I love you' tossed around left and right only to discover the people did not even know the true definition of love. I have experienced the betrayal of adultery. I have experienced the betrayal of those who have walked alongside me, sharing in support and encouragement as they witnessed kingdom building taking place yet when no one was looking were kicking out and removing foundational bricks behind my back. I have experienced the betrayal of thievery as financial resources and intellectual property was taken and sold right out from under my nose. I have been mocked and lied about by those who I considered close confidants in my journey. I have sat with, cried with, held others in my arms, poured time and energy into others, sacrificed financially to help support them when my own home was in need and yet was betrayed.

In some instances the expiration date on connections and/or relationships came to pass but out of emotion or attachment, relationships stayed connected beyond their time table in my life. When a removal, attachment, or severing took place it was packaged as a betrayal when in all reality in those stags of life we both held on longer than we should have.

> *Check the expiration date on some of your connections.*

A word of advice: Do not hold to things past the expiration date or beyond your grace to handle it because you will cause betrayal or the appearances of such to occur when in all reality it could have been avoided. When we see the expiration date on a gallon of milk we are very careful not to drink it. Sometimes we convince ourselves that the milk is still good and we can drink it. But the moment you pour that tall glass of milk out what you see and experience is stench, rot, and curdled milk. It is no longer good. The milk itself didn't do anything wrong, but it did warn you. It did tell you when it was going to expire. It is your responsibility to pay attention to the signs. If you make the choice to hang on to it longer than you should it is going to spoil and could even make you sick. Do not hang on longer then the expiration date in your relationships and connections along your life's journey.

Dearest worshipper, betrayal is unavoidable. It is a part of life in which everyone will experience in some manner-however great or small. You dear one, determine the outcome in how you handle it. Are you going to lash back in vengeance? Are you going to shore your defenses and prove your side from the mountain tops? Or perhaps you will blast your woes and victim mentality all over social media with the hopes of rallying troops to 'your side'. No! This is not the way at all. Emotions and feelings are real and shouldn't be denied. The manner in which you choose to react to them is one choice you are going to have to make. If we are to emulate Christ in our daily living, then even a kiss from Judas should not take us over the edge or completely out of character.

Go ahead and cry, scream, and get mad. But, do it before the Lord. Cast all your care on Him. He's strong. Trust me. He can handle it. He is waiting to receive it from you.

Steer clear of gossip, slander, and murmuring. When you experience this type of thing in your life, steer clear of it ALL the time and shut it down if it comes your way. Oftentimes in this type of scenario it is so easy to fall into the trap of "I'm just venting", or "I need someone to talk it out with", or the best one is "Let's pray about this together" but I am really just trying to put the stamp of HOLY on my gossip filled mouth. There is nothing wrong with expressing yourself in a safe trustworthy environment with someone you know will hold you accountable, but what is not okay is using people as a platform to gossip and slander others all the while you try to mask that garbage in a cloak of falsehood and conniving behaviors. At the end of the day it is going to start to stink because garbage is garbage no matter how you want to dress it up.

Trying to poison others minds about whom betrayed so you have allies is wrong. No Bueno ☺ (means 'no good' in Spanish). You are fooling yourself and allowing the enemy to have a filed day with your life. Stop it! Stop playing victim also during instances when you find yourself as the betrayer. Yes, I said it. Admit you have been on the side of betrayer. What was the root cause which pushed you to betray? Was it jealousy or competition, difference of opinion, dishonor, etc.? What caused you to betray? What choice did you make which lined up with the actions you took? We have all been there.

Now back to Judas. Thank God for the Judas in your life. The one who walked with you, talked with you, did life with you, dreamed dreams with you, and then kissed your check to betray you for a few pieces of silver. Go ahead and thank God! Why? How?

I am so grateful to the multiple kisses I have received from 1...2...3...4...5 Judases in my life because it propelled me in my destiny just as it did for Jesus. It made me look more at my own heart, character, and mindset and drove me deeper in my prayer and worship before God because there was no alternative. The kiss allowed me to seek God more intentionally about who He was to me and I to Him. The sealing of my truest identity in Christ came closer to the surface with each kiss of betrayal.

Believe it or not, after the initial shockwaves of pain or hurt, it pressed me to seek God for greater love, mercy, and compassion for His children. I truly learned how to love more intensely because of the processing of my own heart and character through it all. I did NOT feel this way or think this way the fist time I went through it. I did not even get to a level of maturation enough after the second or third time. But God's grace IS sufficient and His power does work best in my weakness. I clung to 2 Corinthians 12:9, Hebrews 10:36, Psalm 38:8-9, Psalm 50:15 and Isaiah 26:3 relentlessly during these times of the process. God didn't mastermind betrayal for me but He did foreknow them. He used what satan intended for evil-to break me, tear my heart apart, tempt me to curse or walk away from God, destroy my mind, act out recklessly with my life and my body and my activities, and cause hovoc in every part of my life-and God turned it around for good. He glorified Himself in every situation and still does to this day.

No matter what I experienced, endured, had done to me, or had to live through, the Word of the Lord kept me. Along with the scriptures I listed above, the following kept me through it all. The Lord took me to His word when I would sit before Him crying my eyes out and He would comfort me. This is how I fought my battles.

The bible says:
Psalm 24:5 "They will receive the LORD's blessing and have a right relationship with God their savior."

Psalm 89:18 "You crushed the great sea monster. You scattered your enemies with your mighty arm."

Psalm 4:2-4 (My favorite one ☺) "How long will you [allow] people [to] ruin my reputation? How long will you make groundless accusations? How long will you continue your lies? You can be sure of this: The LORD set apart the godly for himself. The LORD will answer when I call to him. Don't sin by letting anger control you. Think about it overnight and remain silent."

Isaiah 50:8 "He who gives me justice is near. Who will dare to bring charges against me now? Where are my accusers? Let them appear!"

Isaiah 54:17 "But in that coming day no weapon turned against you will succeed. You will silence every voice raised up to accuse you. These benefits are enjoyed by the servants of the LORD; their vindication will come from me.
I, the LORD, have spoken!"

He defends, protects, covers, and vindicates us. Pray always. Praise Him at all times. Worship Him continuously no matter what and then stand back and watch Him work. He will do it! He is faithful and His love for us is relentless.

Our response determines the overall reactions as mentioned before. How we choose to respond determines everything.

We often respond to abandonment or betrayal first in an angry manner by dwelling on and rehearsing the circumstance. We often seek to get even or make our betrayers suffer intensely for how badly they have wronged us. Through Jesus's example, we see a proper way to handle betrayal.

We read in the book of Hebrews that Jesus understands all we experience, encounter and are tempted in, yet He did not sin. We also know Jesus's internal struggle is not recorded but we can only assume it was emotionally challenging. He knew what Judah would do and loved him anyway. He didn't try to stop him, fight him, or throw a fit and make a big scene. We see Him respond to Judah with grace. Jesus is by no means a pushover at all, but his <u>response</u> to the betrayal was cloaked in kindness and graciousness. If you have been betrayed or when you will be betrayed in the future, the first and best response is to cry out to Jesus who loves you and intimately understands every detail and reality of what you are experiencing.

Think for a moment how Jesus must have felt. He was turned over into the hands of Jewish religious leaders by someone close to Him. Imagine just briefly the mental anguish caused by his disciple and close friend. This was a part of Jesus suffering too. He had invested in Judas. He loved Judas. He cared intensely for Judas. He was discouraged. He was hurt. He felt pain. He wept intensely. His response was just like ours is today in our moments of betrayal. What kind of internal anguish did He feel knowing the reality of having been sold out? The same anguish we feel too. He felt it. He knows dear one-He knows.

What can we learn from Judas as a betrayer in order to avoid becoming one?

Firstly, when we even hear the name Judas our reaction is a negative association. Judas carries betrayal in the name. What does your name carry when it is spoken? What is the first reaction people have when they hear the sound of YOUR name? There is so much to learn from Judas. If you want to avoid becoming a betrayer, the bible will give you the sound truth you need. Here are the top three ways I have found in my journey from the perspective of betraying along the way and being betrayed. I didn't understand my actions were betrayal until Holy Spirit checked my heart and showed me what He found inside there. Yes beloved, I have been on both sides of this and so I have experience and understanding from both sides. Thank God we have the redeeming power of the cross to cleanse, forgive, and set free!

1. <u>Not Dealing with Frustrations Lead to Betrayal</u>

Those who proclaim Christ as Savior and walk with God but then turn turn away or become apathetic and complacent only become that way through a process. When we choose not to deal with frustrations in our walk with the Lord, our relationships and friendships, and in ministry setting-no matter how great or how small-bitterness creeps in and set the stage for betrayal. In John 12:3-6 we see Judas have a strong opinion against what the woman did. He was frustrated with what he felt Jesus wasn't doing about the situation. All the while he was criticizing Jesus Judas was stealing money behind the scenes. In Matthew 26:14-16 we see Judas is very calculated. His act of calculating just when to betray Jesus was a process that did not happen overnight. He watched every movement and waited. Judas did not like some of the things Jesus did. He did not agree with how he viewed and handled money. His frustration grew and it was easy for him to become more willing to betray. He betrayed Jesus for some chump change. For the meager cost of a slave Judas agreed to betray. Do you really think it was about greed or money? I personally do not believe it to be so. Contrary to what most assume about Judas, I believe he betrayed out of bitterness of heart. It looks like his frustrations grew bigger and bigger over the three years in ministry together with Jesus. He became fed up with the expectations he had of Jesus constantly not being met. To him, Jesus had wasted one to many dollars, he rebuked Judas one to many times, he was tired of being mocked by religious leaders for following Jesus-who appeared to be a crazy leader. So, he betrayed Jesus.

His kiss was sadistic in nature. He could have pointed at him. He could have called out His name and had Him respond. But no, he got close enough for Jesus to feel His breath on His skin as the kiss of a death sentence brushed His check with Judas's lips. How did he get so bitter? How was he so blinded by offense and disgust towards Jesus to do this?

Undealt frustrations always eventually boil over or blow up. Pretending there isn't a problem is a sure fire pre-requisite for betrayal. These things do not happen overnight. People betray one another once the frustrations are too much to handle because they were never really dealt with properly. The bible says in Ephesians 4:26-27 "And "don't sin by letting anger control you. Don't let the sun go down while you are still angry, for anger gives a foothold to the devil". This scripture is very clear why it is not a good idea to hold onto things. Bitterness and anger will grow and develop inside of you if you do not release it.

Like anyone who betrays, Judas couldn't take it anymore. His own pent up frustrations and emotions were never properly dealt with and he chose to do something about it no matter how sinful it was. He let things get so bad he eventually betrayed Jesus to death because he was in denial about his own sin.

Have you ever been frustrated or fed up with leaders in ministry because you felt they should do things differently or see other people's perspectives? Can you see from this example that Judas feelings were real-they were his own, but they were wrong? He should have talked it out with Jesus. He could have also yielded to the Lord even if he did not agree with Him 100 percent and in turn still bring honor to the Lord, the relationship, and the ministry.

2. To Avoid Betrayal, We Must Realize There Are Only three Response to Sin

Matthew 27:3-5 says "When Judas, who had betrayed him, realized that Jesus had been condemned to die, he was filled with remorse. So he took the thirty pieces of silver back to the leading priests and the elders. "I have sinned," he declared, "for I have betrayed an innocent man." "What do we care?" they retorted. "That's your problem." Then Judas threw the silver coins down in the Temple and went out and hanged himself."The bible says a lot about betrayal but the three general responses to sin in our lives are: denial, despair, or repentance. We should want our response to be the latter.

If someone has not repented and is not yet completely crushed by the own sin it is because they are in denial and refuse to believe how bad the sin really is. When repentance does not occur but the person can no longer deny how horrible their sinfulness is, despair usually set in and they can no longer live under the heavy weight of condemnation. The only and best solution is to be quick to repent and receive grace and forgiveness. To avoid becoming a betrayer we have to regularly repent of our sins.

When we can finally come face to face with our inner sinfulness that is the very root of our sin, we only have the three options listed above. We can <u>deny</u> our sin, we can <u>commit suicide</u> like Judas, or we can <u>repent</u> of our sinfulness. Christ is our only hope! How are you or have your responded to the exposure of your own sin? Denial, death, or repentance?

3. Embrace God's Pre-Ordained Reality

The Bible teaches us betrayal is always the result when we refuse to obey God's will and fight for our own. To be a disciple who endures to the end, doesn't betray God, doesn't betray our spouses, doesn't betray our friends, doesn't betray our co-workers or ministry partners, and doesn't betray those we love, we must be disciples who submit to the will of God. Does any of this mean that God caused Judas to sin? Absolutely not. The bible tells us in James 1:13-15 God is never responsible for our sin and we alone are. But throughout the Bible what we do see is God directing man's sin to accomplish God's will.

You will never find a Bible verse where God takes a righteous man, a person trying to please him, and then God uses that man to sin in a certain way to produce what God wanted. However, you will find many instances where someone was already living in sin and rebelling against God, and then God directed that man's steps to sin in a certain way to accomplish a certain outcome that God wanted from the beginning.

When the bible talks about the scriptures having to be fulfilled concerning Judas, it does not mean that God merely predicted the sins of Judas, and although he did not produce the sins of Judas either, by his great power and sovereignty he did direct Judas' sin so that the end result was what God wanted.

And so what does this all have to do with betrayal?

It simply means that to try to fight against the sovereign God is pointless. None of this means that our actions are pointless, that we are robots doing what God wants. It means that your actions are your own but God has a plan that he is going to accomplish, and you are either going to be a part of that plan one way or the other. Fighting against God's preordained reality is pointless. No matter how hard you try, your will is not going to overcome God's will. All you will accomplish in betraying God's way for your own way is your own demise and condemnation.

The bible tells us in Matthew 27:6-10 "The chief priests picked up the coins and said, "It is against the law to put this into the treasury, since it is blood money." So they decided to use the money to buy the potter's field as a burial place for foreigners. That is why it has been called the Field of Blood to this day. Then what was spoken by Jeremiah the prophet was fulfilled: "They took the thirty pieces of silver, the price set on him by the people of Israel, and they used them to buy the potter's field, as the Lord commanded me."

Imagine this scene for a moment. They pick up the thirty pieces of silver that was used as payment to arrange an assassination of an innocent man, but rather than be grief stricken by their murderous acts, all they are concerned about is following the letter of the law. Judas and these Pharisees were able to murder Jesus because they had allowed their relationship with God to turn into a fake religion rather than a true relationship with the living God. They just murdered someone, but now they won't put blood money into the treasurer. If this isn't a fake spirituality I don't know what is.

Throughout all of these horrible actions of Judas and these Pharisees, I believe they forgot one thing. They forgot one thing which allowed them to feel like they could do whatever they wanted. They forgot one thing that made them feel they could kill an innocent man. They forgot one thing that caused them to forsake a genuine relationship with God for a fake, sinful religious, hypocritical lifestyle where the focus was on obeying the letter of the law rather than the Spirit behind the laws. They forgot three little words that can transform us into disciples who endure to the end.

God is real.

If you want to be a person who doesn't betray Jesus, if we want to be a spouses who doesn't betray our wives or husbands, if we want to be friends who don't betray our friendships, if we want to be ministry partners or kingdom builders who don't betray our brothers and sisters in Christ, if want to be a parent who doesn't betray your children, if you want to be a man or woman that when you fail, you always repent and turn back to Christ – then we have to remember this truth that Judas the betrayer clearly forgot.

God is real.

This isn't a game. This isn't about making money, being a prestigious religious figure, having titles or positions, or about experiencing as much earthly pleasure while there's time. Life is about glorifying God and enjoying him forever because HE IS REAL.

"Betrayal is a plan of the enemy to stop you from what God would have for you. It is a low blow. It is an emotional attack. It is an attempt to throw a chain of sorrow around you and keep you right where you are or to send you backwards."-Jennifer Eivaz

"One of the biggest things I've learned about overcoming betrayal is that you have to have your identity in God before you have your identity in anyone else. Betrayal will come, but it carries a dual purpose and comes as the "sifter." It sifts wrong people out of your life, but it also sifts out your true heart identity." –Jennifer Eivaz

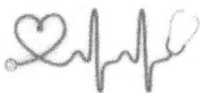

Heart Check Up

What areas of your life have you experienced betrayal? What made it FEEL like a betrayal?

_____

_____

_____

_____

What steps are you going to take to relinquish the desire for vengeance to the Lord?

_____

_____

_____

_____

Are there areas in your life where you know you have been the betrayer? If so, what caused you to get to that place?

_____

_____

_____

_____

What changes are you going to make today in order to walk in a state of repentance versus denial or death?

_____

_____

_____

_____

Prayer for the betrayed: Father, in the name of Jesus I stand before your presence. I am coming to you God because I have felt the sting of betrayal and it hurts God. My heart is overwhelmed with rejection, pain, sadness, and despair (add your own emotions here as you see fit). I don't want to be this way anymore God. I give over every emotion, thought, and feeling I have been carrying and I cast it onto you. Help me Lord to release all that torments me through this betrayal. Give me a heart of love and compassion for those who have betrayed me and teach me to love them like you do. Set me free from this prison in my mind and allow me to walk in freedom. Bathe me in your love, grace, and mercy. I lift my betrayers up to your feet Lord and I ask that you would be merciful to them. Bring them into the light and show them the way so that they to may be free. I let them go and set them free from being captive in my own mind and ask Lord that you would bless them. Thank you Lord for hearing my cry to you. Thank you Lord for setting me free. Thank you Lord for loving me.

Prayer for the betrayer: Father, in the name of Jesus, I am coming before you to repent. Forgive me for the sin in my life. Forgive me for entertaining thoughts of anger, bitterness, resentment, jealously, and competition (add your own thoughts/actions here as you see fit) I have denied for far to long that anything was wrong. I have allowed spiritual death to creep into my life and my heart and it has gone on for far too long. I repent Lord and I receive your forgiveness. Please restore, right, and renew the relationships that I have been a part of destroying. Restore, right, and renew the friendships, families, partnerships, ministries, colleagues, and all relationships I have been a part of tearing down or destroying due to my own sin. Thank you for exposing my heart and showing me what is inside. Clean it out Lord. Do whatever it takes to make me whole again and remove what is not pleasing to you from my heart. I receive your love. I receive your forgiveness. I receive your peace. I pray for those I have betrayed and ask that you would mend their hearts as well. Remove the anguish and pain and restore your love, hope, freedom and joy to their lives. You are God alone and I know that you can and will do all these things. I thank you.

9 SEVEN LETTERS OF SHAME
D I V O R C E

There is not one little girl on the face of the planet who sits and dreams about getting divorced. Most little girls play with Barbie and Ken and dream wildly as they create a beautiful picture of love and marriage in their own imaginations. Many little girls have this innate desire to play "mommy & baby" and spend their playtimes nurturing, caring for, feeding, dressing, and changing their little bundle of joy. Little girls are taught to become wives and mothers from very early on. Toy manufacturers have made billions in catering to the idealism of girls as moms and wives and boys as builders and protectors. They are not to far off.

When God created Adam it was first for relationship, then to lead, build, protect. He created Eve as his helper who also bore children, raised and nurtured them along his side. Eve was to support, assist, care for, and love Adam as she loved God. They, together, were made to worship God and to experience intimacy with Him on a daily basis. Toymakers for 100's of years have hit the jackpot in this area. As these little girls and boys grow in stature and maturity and enter into relationships, we now see divorce lawyers hitting that same pool of the jackpot as they cater to the crushing and traumatic episodes of divorce all over the world.

When young girls sit and play dress up, wedding day, and baby care they don't dream disaster. To the contrary, their hearts and minds are fixed on the fairytales of prince charming and their happily ever after.

Mine were. I can remember playing by myself as a little girl and dreaming about who I would be when I grew up, who my prince charming would be, the wedding day bliss, the gorgeous house we would call our home, 6 children – yes 6 and I had all their names picked out too. We would be so in love and so happy. We would grow old together like my grandparents and leave a legacy behind. Sadly these things did not entirely come to pass. Never in my life of daydreaming neither as a little girl nor through adulthood could someone have told me I would eventually be stamped with the pen of shame in big red letters with the word D I V O R C E. Never in a million years would I have believed it. But it happened. It happened to me. It broke me in a million pieces and changed my life forever.

D-oes not happen overnight
I-nduces excruciating pain
V-ictim mentality
O-stracizes you
R-adically changes everything
C-auses mental anguish
E-radicates the original design for the family unit

Reread that. It is all very true. Divorce does not happen overnight. It is something that builds and builds over time. Neither person wants to admit they had anything to do with it or take the blame but it takes two people to come to terms with the fact that it is indeed happening and they both have a part to play. The act of divorce induces excruciating pain for both people. When there are children involved the pain increases 100 fold. The pain divorce creates is insurmountable. Divorce will also cause people to fall into a victim mentality. Each person can take on the "I was the victim in all of this" or "It was all her/his fault". When this happens the victim mentality will begin to feed you more and more lies about who you are, who you are not, where you failed, what went wrong, how you destroyed everything, etc. and you will find yourself feeling victimized over and over again. Divorce can and does ostracize you. Relationships you had as a couple have now become awkward or non-existent because of people"s own personal opinions or lies they feed into and believe. You begin to feel as if you are all alone and there is no one who can even understand what you are experiencing.

Divorce will isolate you and almost imprison you in your own thoughts of loss, having no self-worth or value, and the overwhelming desperation of wanting to just be normal again. Divorce will definitely radically change your entire life. All aspects of your life as you knew it will totally flip upside down and inside right. Divorce will cause severe mental anguish. Your thought life is an area where the spirit of divorce will have a field day and fill your mind with lie after lie after lie and literally enjoy torturing you through your thoughts. Divorce eradicates the original design for the family unit hands down. God doesn't like divorce. In fact the bible says He hates divorce. He did not intend for his children to come together and create families to then in turn destroy them or tear them apart-No! He loves family. He did after all give us the perfect design for family.

How do I know the effects of divorce? I experienced this for myself. After being together with someone for 22 years and married for 17 I found myself allowing a mere signature on a sheet of paper determine my marriage covenant and family was being severed apart. I will NEVER forget the day as long as I live.

When the day finally came to sign our divorce documents I can remember "This isn't happening for real. This is going to get fixed. When we see each other everything will be okay and this will all feel like a bad dream." I pulled up to the office we had to meet at and was shaking like a leaf. My heart was pounding inside of my chest so hard I thought it would literally explode. I could't even get out of my car. My phone rang and it was him. We both sat on the phone talking for over an hour trying to figure out what went so horribly wrong. We still could not agree on how to fix it and so when he finally arrived I had to muster up the courage to get out of my car. We entered this office and I felt like I was in a nightmare watching myself from afar. The gentlemen in front of us pulled out our documents and we looked at each other one last time as if asking with our eyes "should we really do this". I think at this point we were both so far gone in our minds we had no idea how to get back and we just answered each other silently. One pen stroke after another after another after another after another and it was finally done. We walked out of this office together headed towards the parking lot until we reached our cars. We turned and looked at each other again once more and then embraced each other and sobbed and sobbed in each other's arms as we mourned the death of our marriage that day. I do not even know how long we stood there in each other's arms weeping and wailing together. You could literally feel the destruction of covenant taking place. It is the most painful thing any human can experience. When we were finally able to tear apart from each other it just seemed as if we had gone so far there was no turning back at that point. After all, the documents were not mailed yet. We could have torn them up right then and there. But, we didn't. Pride got in the way for both of us. We both wanted to be right and prove the hurt caused by the other person was worse. And so, we walked away from each other and didn't look back again.

I drove to the post office and dropped the envelope in the receptacle and just began screaming and screaming all by myself in the car. I couldn't even breathe. I was shattered in pieces. I drove to a local park, parked my car and just sat for several hours crying, and screaming and asking God why. Later that evening, we ended up speaking on the phone for several hours again trying to figure out what happened and how we got to the place we were in. Neither one of us could see what the other saw. We were so blinded by our own desires to be healed and be right we couldn't hear what the other person was saying at all. I felt I was never enough and could never be who he wanted me to be and he felt he was in competition with my relationship with God and that he could never be enough for me either. Why God WHY?! I thought I did everything I could. I fasted, I prayed, I fasted some more. I anointed every crack, crevice, and corner of my home several times. I had trusted intercessors come to my home when he was away to battle in prayer in my home and over my marriage bed-literally-to try to salvage it. I stayed and wanted everything to be okay between us. I didn't always agree with my husband's ways or thoughts, but I wanted to try to make things better. I pursued God and sought Him for answers. I worshipped harder and deeper than I ever had before and yet I still ended up divorced.

I loved my husband very much. I cannot every say I didn't or that he didn't love me. As you read earlier we were two broken kids trying to fix our brokenness through each other rather than allowing ourselves to become two whole people in Christ who then come together wholly then as one. I wanted an escape and he wanted to be loved and adored. It worked for us for a time.

I received several warning messages before I got married from different people in my life advising me to walk away from the relationship because it was not good for me. I had a prophet come to warn me of the dangerous road I was walking down and he implored me to step off the road I was traveling. I refused to listen. He paid attention to me, he picked me, and he showed me what I thought was love at the time so it had to be right. I never asked God. I never once said is this your will. I didn't invite him into the situation at all.

God doesn't force us into or out of anything. We have our own free will to decide things. His warnings were sent to help prevent years of heartache and pain, but I chose to be deaf to them all. If I walked away would anyone else really want me? I was too insecure and afraid to even thinking about waiting for anyone else. I was his. He loved me and we began to build a life together regardless of the fact we were building on a faulty foundation and it was bound to topple eventually.

Yes, there was a lot of heartache, betrayal, adultery, lies, manipulation, and abuse on both our parts. But, we did experience happy moments. We have four gorgeous children who are the joy of our lives. We made tons of great memories together and there were really good times. However, the scars from the bad seemed to just drown out the good. Again, it did not happen overnight. This built up for years and years. Undealt with and unresolved issues just got bigger and bigger and our individual brokenness was never really mended. So, we were still two broken people trying to act whole. But the brokenness was still there tucked under the carpet where no one could see until one day the items tucked under the carpet got so big we had a mountain before us. We tried biblical counseling and for a season in our marriage it helped to bring some healing and restoration but it was short lived as we ended up back in the same old habits together.

The trauma of divorce affected us, our children, our family, our friends, our job, the ministry, our finances, our relationships, and so much more. But I am thankful. What? How can I say this? It took me almost four years to be able to say that I am thankful. I am thankful because it took this trauma to take me to place deep in the heart of God that I had not been before. I worshipped and prayed for my life because I was literally contending for my life. I had nothing else to turn to. I had no one else to turn to. It was just me and Jesus. Me and Jesus. Me and Jesus. I finally got to know areas of His heart for me that I hadn't known before. It was brought on by the need for me to cry out to scream out in a very raw and really way before my Abba. He was it. I worshipped my way through the trauma. I worshipped my way through the stages of death and mourning because that is exactly what I was experiencing. I had to spend time on my knees and most often my my face planted to the ground before the Lord crying desperately for Him to heal me, rescue me, to help me. I worshipped before, yes. I prayed and interceded before, yes. But THIS drove me to such a deep, deep place into the Lord's arms and heart that I had never been. In that place He healed me. In that place He showed me how He was my husband. In that place He revealed Himself to me as Father, my Abba. In that place, He revealed Himself to me as provider, protector, way maker, life sustainer, miracle worker. In that place, He showed me exactly how He sees me and how beautiful and precious I am to Him and how He ran to the front of the line to pick … me. Yeah beloved reader, He picked me. He chose me. He did it with a relentless passion for me.

He showed me just how He thought about me when He was being nailed to the cross. He whispered my name …'Reyna' and He said "It is all for you. I love you and I choose you. You are mine and I am yours." I could see His face and I could sense His immense love for me in that very moment. He knew all my sin and yet He still picked me and chose to die for me to redeem all of it.

Christ romanced me back to life again. He took me through a process-yes. He romanced me whole. I was finally able to look at myself in the mirror and not see brokenness but see a wholly redeemed queen looking back at herself. I was finally able to identify with the Christ inside myself and understand who I was to Him and who He was in me. I thought I knew. I only knew in part. It took this…this stamping of myself with the 7 letters of shame to realize just what He created in me and how He truly designed me to be.

The Lord eventually even helped to experience an agape love for my now ex-husband. I didn't want to love him anymore. I didn't want him to be able to control my emotions or have a hold over me anymore. I absolutely didn't want to LOVE him because it hurt too much to still love him. But Holy Spirit got a hold of me and told me one day "I am going to teach you to see him with the eyes of love just like the Father does." I was blown away. How could I? I experienced so much hurt and pain I couldn't bear to think about allowing this, but my desire to obey the Lord far outweighed my desire to do my own thing. So, I yielded to the process of allowing God to show me how to love him like he does. Over time I slowly began to have immense love in my heart for him, but it wasn't the husband/wife type of love it was like agape love. Agape love is talked about in the Word along with Phileo love. They are vastly different. He wasn't asking me to Phileo him, He was asking me to develop, nurture, and express agape love toward him.

Phileo love is: to have fondness or a friendship with
Agape love is: to love dearly, to be well pleased with.

The first love called "phileo" love and that is the love that the city of Philadelphia was named after…brotherly love. This type of love is what friends have for one another. This type of **love** can also exist between brothers and sisters, aunts and uncles and other family members but it is most frequently associated with a deep, abiding friendship. This is a love that is shared between the best of friends, much like that of King David and Jonathan, King Saul's son. It is, or at least should be, the type of love that exists between church members. It is a love that is not passionate like that between a husband and a wife. After Jesus resurrection He came to the disciples and He asked Peter, if he loved Him. The word Jesus used about whether Peter loved Him was "agapao" but Peter must have been caught off guard and said "Yes Lord, you know that I love you" (John 21:15) but the word Peter used was the Greek "phileo" which is the brotherly love. Peter didn't get it. Jesus was using the strongest of all types of love, agape.

Here are some Scriptures that use the word agape. The type of love expressed in the bible in John 3:16 is the type of love which is always the highest, most supreme love there it. It is a love where one is willing to die for another, even if that person is unworthy, sinful, undeserving and is an enemy of the one who died for them.

First John 4:8 "Anyone who does not love (agape) does not know God, because God is love (agape)."

Romans 5:5 "and hope does not put us to shame, because God's love (agape) has been poured into our hearts through the Holy Spirit who has been given to us."

John 10:17 "For this reason the Father loves (agape) me, because I lay down my life that I may take it up again."

Second Peter 1:17 "For when he received honor and glory from God the Father, and the voice was borne to him by the Majestic Glory, "This is my beloved (agapetos) Son, with whom I am well pleased."

John 21:20 "Peter turned and saw the disciple whom Jesus loved (agapao) following them, the one who also had leaned back against him during the supper and had said, "Lord, who is it that is going to betray you?"

Agape love is the kind of love that God had for us, while we were still dead in our sins. Agape love is a God love. This love is a love that Jesus displayed in laying down His life voluntarily for us; the type of love that the Father and Jesus have for One another; a love that is poured out for us like Jesus' blood was poured out for sinners.

And so Jesus was asking me, Reyna, to open my heart to receive more agape from Him in order for me to see my ex-husband through those eyes. The eyes of burning love just like the Father has for us.

He did it. He gave it to me and now when I see him, I can see who Christ sees. I no longer see the hurt. I no longer see the past. I just simply see him like Jesus does and realize he is so loved by God and is His son. He's seen through the eyes of love.

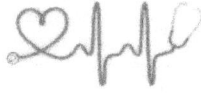

Heart Check Up

Have you or someone you know experienced the trauma of divorce? What parts of your heart need to be repaired because of the breech in covenant? Hand them over to the Lord.

_____

_____

_____

_____

Perhaps you are in the middle of contemplating divorce now. Write down all the reasons you should fight for your marriage. Write down all the reasons you feel you should give up. Now, yield them to the Lord and trust Him to repair and restore what seems irreparable. Seek Godly counsel and know that Christ can right every wrong. He is the mender of hearts and wants to be invited into mending yours.

_____

_____

_____

_____

Perhaps you have a healthy, strong and striving marriage OR you are single. Awesome! Pray for those who are going through a difficult time and are struggling. Go before the Lord on their behalf and storm heaven for their marriages.

Please know if you or someone you know is in a dangerous situation or being severely abused in any manner, they are by no means implored to remain in that environment. But healing and restoration can even come to those situations when handled in a manner where everyone is in a safe environment and counsel is sought to help both parties reconcile in a healthy and safe manner. If this is not feasible, seek your pastor's guidance as to how to move forward. There is no quick fix or cookie cutter solution which fits every scenario. I can only speak from a place and share with you what I experienced and learned from with the Lord by my side through ti all.

Prayer: Father God in Heaven, I come before you in the name of Jesus and I first and foremost repent for allowing and entertaining the thoughts of divorce or separation to enter my thought life. You are the God who heals, redeems, renews, and restores. I trust you God and I know that you have a plan and a purpose for my life. Your plan is one that is good and not one that plans evil or harm. I trust your Word and believe you will turn every situation in my life that was intended for evil into good. I lift my spouse _____ to you God and ask that you would help both of us to yield our own agendas to your feet. Helps us Lord to walk through the steps of redemption and restoration for your glory. Help us to let our walls down and let our guard down so that we can see and hear each other as you do. Heal what the enemy has intended to kill and rebuild what He has tried to destroy. I trust you God. Help me even when I don't trust myself. Help us both to open our hearts to receive your healing and may our story of redemption be one of great testimony to encourage and exhort others you will bring across our path to help along the journey of healing. I bless you Lord and I thank you Oh God of restoration for hearing me this day. I believe I will see it all turn around and I will give testimony because of it. You are an amazing God and I love you!

10 VANITY

the vain one

Vanity manifests itself in many ways. Maybe you may spend too much time worrying about your appearance and your physical beauty. Or perhaps you are consumed by what other people think of you and your reputation. You might be concerned with your status in life and whether or not you appear to be living a seemingly successful life.

Today, we live in a society that is so consumed with self- gratification and glorification that it's hard not to fall prey to vanity. It can be easy to get caught up in this way of living–checking Instagram for how many likes our latest picture got or comparing our social lives to our friends on Facebook. But the reality is, this does not help us in the fight against vanity.

Vanity is sin. How so? It is a sin because we become consumed by other's opinions of our self, rather than concerning ourselves with the opinion of God. Vanity assures us that the cares of the world are more important than those of God. When we begin thinking this way, we are drawn away from God and that's exactly what any sin does, it separates us from God.

I was locked and loaded into that sin wholeheartedly. I LOVED clothes. Shoes. Jewelry. I enjoy shopping and being girlie. I enjoy and look forward to salon time. I mean, what girls doesn't? There was a time though where I was more concerned about the outside than I was about the inside. I had a closet packed with clothes and shoes galore. It was a time I really struggled with my identity. If I could 'look' all put together than things in life would be okay. No one would really know inside I was like a girl trapped in a prison cell banging on the cars screaming for help to be set free, yet there was no sound coming out, no help, ho hope. I had to silence who was really inside. Hurt, rejected, abandoned, self-loathing Reyna.

The outside could have looked as beautifully put together as ever but the inside was a broken mess. How may of us can say we have experience this or are currently walking around this way? Are you walking out the church look? Are you dressed well outside with a façade of this godly person who has it all together when the real deal is you have areas of your life and your heart which need to be healed? What you re hiding from? I hid from many things. I didn't want to appear as if I didn't have a good life, marriage, relationships, enough education, etc. And it all stems back to my struggle I had with an approval addiction, low self-worth, and a lack of identity.

I had a severe case of vainglory (vanity). Vainglory defined is: inordinate pride in oneself or ones' achievements; excessive vanity. I definitely could have won major awards in this category. My vanity was also packaged very nicely with pride and arrogance. I really thought I was IT. ☺ Thank God for His loving ways in which He redirects us!

Why was all this necessary? In my mind, if I looked beautiful than I would be accepted. If I was accepted enough by how I was viewed on the outside, perhaps someone would take the time to even get to know or value what I had inside. My mind was quite warped in its thinking pattern but it came from years and years of the enemy lying to me and taunting me over and over again.

There came a point in my walk with the Lord where I was tired of being fake. I wanted to just be me. I was me before Him when we were alone so why couldn't I be me in public. He wanted the real Reyna he created to stand up everywhere she went and no longer put the fake one on for others.

One day He asked me if I loved Him enough to trust Him with what He was going to ask me to do. I hesitantly mustered a 'yes' from my lips because I knew it was going to be a hard task but I had to trust Him that it would be worth it. He asked me to give everything away. What? You can't be serious. But, oh He was. I gave it all away. Everything. All of it. He allowed me to keep 2 pair of shoes, 1 pair of jeans, 1 pair of slacks, 1 simple dress, and 2 tops. I lived that way for 2 years. I gave away garbage bags and totes FULL of clothes, shoes, jewelry, etc. and remained with, what for me, was the most humbling remnant of a wardrobe ever. It was so hard. It was so humbling yet so worth it. It was the beginning of a process of my heart surgery to remove vainglory/vanity from it.

He did it though. I surrendered and yielded to the process of breaking off vanity, pride, false-humility, arrogance, and the fakeness. He took all of that and began to teach me what humility truly is and how my worth and value didn't come from what I looked liked but it came from Him. He promised me He would restore what I had and to even greater measure than before and I trusted Him at His word.

When I finally got to a place where I didn't care anymore if I spent the rest of my life with the meager wardrobe I had left and I didn't even think about it anymore, it was then He began to restore. He sent people on several separate occasions to come to take me on shopping sprees. They would each separately say "the Lord sent me to take you shopping. Get whatever you want." Or, they would show up on my doorstep with bags and bags of brand new clothes and shoes and jewelry. He did it. When I didn't need it anymore to validate who I was, He gave it back to me and even better!

He dressed me well. He took care of me and still does to this day. I will still have moments where I just have the thought "It would be nice to have a new dress or shirt, but I am grateful for all that you have given me Lord. Thank you!" Seriously, moments later I will get a phone call or text from someone saying "time to go shopping" or I will get a package that says "the Lord said this is for you" and it will contain exactly what I thought about. I don't even have to ask Him at all. He already knows and lavishes me again and again.

Overcoming vanity, like any sin, takes time, effort, perseverance, and of course, the grace of God. But I've found these three daily habits helped in my pursuit of His presence over my need for man's approval or affirmation.

1. Confession and Repentance

When we are in a continual mindset of confessing and repenting when we feel vanity creeping its way into our hearts and minds we open ourselves up for the Lord to redirect us each time. We also allow ourselves to be teachable and moldable by Him so we can change daily to be more and more like Him.

2. Pray

Be in constant dialogue with God. He knows all of your thoughts already, so you might as well be honest with Him! If you are struggling with body image, or what other people think of you, turn it over to God in prayer. Ask Him for the grace to grow in the virtue of humility and be prepared to be humbled! Pray to be free from the fears of judgement, free from the bonds of perfectionism, free from the fear of other people's opinions of you.

3. Read the Word

We are responsible to renew our minds daily and this will help redirect and refocus our minds as we spend time in the Word. It is there you will find direction, answers, refreshing and guidance towards where your thoughts should be aligned in lieu of focusing on yourself. The Word will wash over you and help to renew you.

4. Worship

Worship places complete focus on Jesus. In the secret place with Him you love on Him and He loves on you. It is in that place you can see yourself as He sees you. When you are in that intimate exchange and focused on just bringing delight and pleasure to the Lord, there is no time or room for you to worry about yourself or the opinions of others. You are totally engulfed in the beauty of His face and the passion of His heart for you. Worship will redirect your need for things to be all about you because you have to prostrate yourself humbly before God and focus on Him. At that point, it is NOT about you boo ☺ It is ALL about Him.

The bible says in Philippians 4:11-13 "Not that I was ever in need, for I have learned how to get along happily whether I have much or little. I know how to live on almost nothing or with everything. I have learned the secret of living in every situation, whether it is with a full stomach or empty, with plenty or little. For I can do everything with the help of Christ who gives me the strength I need."

The bible says in Philippians 4:19 "And this same God who takes care of me will supply all your needs from his glorious riches, which have been given to us in Christ Jesus."

Jesus also tells us in Matthew 6:28-33 "And why worry about your clothing? Look at the lilies of the field and how they grow. They don't work or make their clothing, yet Solomon in all his glory was not dressed as beautifully as they are. And if God cares so wonderfully for wildflowers that are here today and thrown into the fire tomorrow, he will certainly care for you. Why do you have so little faith?

"So don't worry about these things, saying, 'What will we eat? What will we drink? What will we wear?' These things dominate the thoughts of unbelievers, but your heavenly Father already knows all your needs. Seek the Kingdom of God above all else, and live righteously, and he will give you everything you need."

Lastly, He always restores ☺. The bible says in Deuteronomy 30:3-13 MSG "God, your God, will restore everything you lost; he'll have compassion on you; he'll come back and pick up the pieces from all the places where you were scattered. No matter how far away you end up, God, you're God, will get you out of there and bring you back to the land your ancestors once possessed. It will be yours again. He will give you a good life and make you more numerous than your ancestors. God, your God, will cut away the thick calluses on your heart and your children's hearts, freeing you to love God, your God, with your whole heart and soul and live, really live. God, your God, will put all these curses on your enemies who hated you and were out to get you. And you will make a new start, listening obediently to God, keeping all his commandments that I'm commanding you today. God, your God, will outdo himself in making things go well for you: you'll have babies, get calves, grow crops, and enjoy an all-around good life. Yes, God will start enjoying you again, making things go well for you just as he enjoyed doing it for your ancestors. But only if you listen obediently to God, your God, and keep the commandments and regulations written in this Book of Revelation. Nothing halfhearted here; you must return to God, your God, totally, heart and soul, holding nothing back."

Thank God He was able to rescue me and deliver me from myself. He truly is amazing.

If you struggle with needing to be seen all put together or with trying to impress man with your outside appearance, surrender those feelings and habits to the Lord. There is nothing wrong with looking cute and feeling beautiful (or handsome for the men out there). Where the sin comes in is when it supersedes your yieldedness before the Lord and it takes your attention away from what truly matters- intimate relationship with the Lord and a lifestyle of worship where He is glorified in everything that you do.

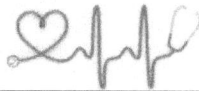

Heart Check Up

Where have you experienced evidence of vainglory/vanity in your life? List them here.

_____

_____

♡ What are you willing to give up in order to make more room for God in your heart?

♡ Identify areas in your life where seed was planted which has caused you to seek approval from man based on the outward more than the inward.

♡ Look in the mirror. What do you see? Write down every positive thing you can see about yourself. Embrace even those which you would consider flaws and speak life and positive affirmations over yourself. Receive the love of God as you do. Ask Him to open your eyes to see yourself as He does.

Prayer: Father God, in the name of Jesus I come before you. I desire to release to you all aspects of vainglory and vanity from my life. I repent Lord for being consumed with myself and for seeking the approval of man far above your approval. Forgive me Lord and I receive your forgiveness. I confess that I have been self-absorbed and self-consumed with my outward appearance as well as the thought of being accepted by others solely based on what I look like, how I carry myself, or by the mindset of what is called 'approved' by man's opinion. Spirit of the living God break off every stronghold that has been built up and taken root in my mind in direct correlation to needing affirmation from man. Spirit of the living God uproot every seed that has taken root in my heart and created a web of entanglement to choke out the source of my real worth and value which is through you. I stand before you and I renounce the spirit of vainglory, vanity, and pride. I ask by the finger of God for every spirit associated with this assignment on my life to remain self-absorbed and unfocused to be driven out in the name of Jesus. I command every spirit assigned to continually torment my mind about not being good enough to be removed from my life immediately. Release your grip now in the name of Jesus. By the blood of Jesus which was shed on the cross for me I am completely accepted and am whole through the blood. I accept and receive your peace, my identity in you, the washing of your Word over me, humility, and reliance and confidence in you alone today. I am accepted. I am loved. I am born of the incorruptible seed of Christ. I am made in your image Jesus. I am a reflection of you. I am called and I am chosen by you. Satan no longer has my permission to operate and I command every access point that I have opened up knowingly and unknowingly to be shut down now in the name of Jesus. I command a spiritual blockage to the communication channels the enemy and his cohorts have had access to in my life and permanently seal off their ability to continue. I shut it down. I shut it down now in the name of Jesus. I paint my mind, my ear gate and my eye gate with the blood of Jesus. Satan you may not cross the bloodline of Jesus that surrounds me and covers me head to toe. Access denied. I decree and declare your access in my life, in my family, in my children, in my bloodline now and in future generations has been denied. Cut off. You are evicted. Get out! Get out! Get out!

Father, send your angels to pick up the word of the Lord and not return to you until it has completed what you set it forth to do. Angels go! Angles go and ride swift on the wind as messengers of the Lord. Thank you for your love, covering, and protection Lord. Thank you for freeing me, restoring, me, and allowing me to see and know who I am in You. Jesus you are Lord of my life and I love you.

11 COMPETITION & JEALOUSY

I will not mince my words in this chapter. Let's just get right to it. Competition in ministry is so ugly! It is detestable to think the people of God feel it necessary to battle, compete and compare themselves to each other as if one over the other would be more pleasing or acceptable to the Lord. Competition and jealousy are breeding grounds for divisiveness, disunity, discord, division, and strife among ministers and ministries. These types of mindsets and behaviors love to have the "look how great I am!" attitude. They also love to compare and justify why their gift, talent, ministry, etc. is so much more deserving than another. They are some who are quite exclusive and deny access to those who simply don't measure up to what they feel is 'good enough' to be a part of. None of this is pleasing to God yet worship arts ministers and ministries are full of people who walk in these ways.

Jealously works hand in hand with competition and comparison. Together, they purpose to wreak havoc on a worship artist's mind which will eventually lead to the defilement of the altar of worship.

When this is entertained and access into the heart is allowed, the heart becomes sick and diseased because of allowing these things to take root. The spirit of jealousy can cause a lot of damage in your church or ministry if it's not dealt with properly. The spirit of jealousy will cause striving and ungodly competitions to flourish.

Gossip, backbiting and pettiness will be evident in a ministry where the spirit of jealousy exists. The bible tells us in Numbers 5:14 about an actual demonic spirit called jealousy, it reads, "If the spirit of jealousy comes on him and he is jealous of his wife." People in leadership can actually develop an atmosphere for this spirit to stir when they are promoting favorites and family members, instead of promoting people based on a their merits and abilities.

The bible says in 2 Corinthians 10:12–13 "They who measure themselves by one another and compare themselves with one another are not wise. But we will not boast beyond measure, but within the boundaries which God has appointed us, which reach even you."

God instructs us not to compare ourselves with others, because that really is just another form of covetousness. When we are watching what others have and we are comparing ourselves to them, we are allowing the spirit of jealousy access to our lives.

2 Corinthians 10:12 tells us that comparing ourselves to others is wrong, and it will cause us to have a jealous spirit if we continue to do that. Faith understands that what God did for one, He will do for another. Romans 2:11 says, "For there is no partiality with God."

We should never despise someone's harvest because we do not know what they have sown to receive it, and the Bible simply says it is not wise to compare with others.

There was a time when I would visit other churches or ministries and even secular arts venues and could feel a pang of jealously because they seemed to be so accomplished, had so many members, had technological advances and access to resources I just wished and dreamed I would have one day. I experienced jealously in relationships, friendships, in the corporate world and in ministry settings. I always felt I needed to be better, have better, do better and those who did excel beyond where I was at the time must have been holding out on something that I just couldn't access. My mind began to play tricks on me and cause me to think things that were not pleasing to the Lord at all and were down right sinful. I would think about what I could do to surpass them, how I could be seen as better or bigger, or how I could get others to join my side against them so that I could be seen as the best. We've talked about this issues in previous chapters so I won't digress, however, I want you dear read to see how all these different things, when not yielded to the Lord, can cause much turmoil in one's life.

But then, Holy Spirit would speak to me and say "rejoice at others' blessings because I will do the same for you and in even greater measure. Just remain faithful and trust me." When we are faced with someone else's prosperity, we are at a crossroads to either covet or decide to be encouraged. We must learn to rejoice at another's blessings because God can do the same thing for us!

Jealousy can literally blind us and cause us to become very angry, bitter, and even lose our minds. King Saul was literally being tormented in his mind to such a degree with jealously that the bible says in 1 Samuel 18:10 …he began to rave like a madman." The Bible says that the Spirit of God departed from Saul when a spirit of jealousy entered him! 1 Samuel 18:12 "for Saul was afraid of him and he was jealous because the Lord had left him and was now with David."

When we allow the spirit of jealousy to enter that spirit will blind us and cause us to stumble.

We need to be careful that a spirit of jealousy does not take hold of us and put out the Spirit's fire on the inside of us!- You don't want the 'wrong' kind of fire to consume you; it can, if you let the spirit of jealousy in.

Rather the word of God says, that we must be consumed by the presence of the LORD and the deep things of God!

There can be much unspoken jealousy in the Body of Christ and especially amongst worship artists. Jealousy brings division and discord. Jealously will also find supporters and pull them along with them on the road to division in the ministry.

There are 6 things I have found jealousy can cause:

1. Jealousy is a devouring spirit.

It will feed insecurity. It is the opposite of faith, because by being jealous of what someone else has, people stop believing in their own destiny that God has purposefully set up for every believer uniquely.

2. Jealousy causes us to envy.

Envy can cause us to covet things that really are not part of our "spiritual design". For example specific gifts, callings, or positions.

Deal with insecurity! Deal with issues that cause jealousy, get healing and move forward. All those things that are meant for us, will come as the Spirit leads in God's timing. Never try to be something or someone you are not! It will always be a struggle!

3. Jealousy closes us off to God's truth.

If jealousy is inside of us, it closes us off to truth. We cannot receive from those over us in the Lord because we will refuse to hear & see them as mentors, but rather we will always be looking to "compete" instead of receiving.

Be sure you are first receiving and standing in agreement with those joined to your ministry, before you draw off or acknowledge voices, a.k.a 'side chatter' on the outside.

When we start acknowledging everyone on the 'outside' before those we are joined in covenant with, and then rarely seem to acknowledge those we are joined to; this is the start of a jealous spirit which leads to a religious spirit because it causes us to be 'selective', picking and choosing what we want to accept or receive including what the Word of God says.

4. Jealousy hardens the heart.

Jealousy has devoured and hardened people's hearts. It causes them to leave ministries, it causes leaders to fragment, and it causes ministries to split simply because its root is pride and insecurity. It also distorts perceptions of self and others. It will create spiritual blindness in not honoring those God has put in our midst to guide and help us. We cannot honor those we envy, or are jealous of! It is a constant struggle.

5. Jealousy is a sign of spiritual immaturity.

Jealousy is a sign of spiritual immaturity because with jealousy we are still seeing things from a worldly perspective.

When we are looking from this perspective we see the 'haves' and 'have-nots' and we are drawing conclusions about how God sees us and loves us from circumstances, not from a point of faith. When we look from a carnal perspective it kills vision.

6. Walk by faith and not by sight.

Being able to receive word, and acknowledge where it comes from is a sign of spiritual maturity. We must walk by faith and not by sight.

Release it to the Lord, repent, and ask the Lord to give you eyes to see. Jesus said love one another, and learn from each other. The more comfortable we are with ourselves, the more we desire to give recognition and honor to the LORD and other people.

Let's take a look at one of the best examples of what NOT to do in ministry. Please do not think so highly of yourself to feel as if you would NEVER do this. Lucifer was literally in the presence of God and he fell. None of us have arrived to a degree where we could say "I would never…" But, pray for the grace and mercy of God to continually cover you, keep you humble, and mindful of how holy our God is and how much you are in need of Him.

The bible says in Ezekiel 28:11-19 "Then this further message came to me from the LORD: "Son of man, sing this funeral song for the king of Tyre. Give him this message from the Sovereign LORD: "You were the model of perfection, [your settings and mountings were made of gold] full of wisdom and exquisite in beauty. You were in Eden, the garden of God. Your clothing was adorned with every precious stone—red carnelian, pale-green periodot, white moonstone, blue-green beryl, onyx, green jasper, blue lapis lazuli, turquoise, and emerald—all beautifully crafted for you and set in the finest gold. They were given to you on the day you were created. I ordained and anointed you as the mighty angelic guardian. You had access to the holy mountain of God and walked among the stones of fire. "You were blameless in all you did from the day you were created until the day evil was found in you. Your rich commerce led you to violence, and you sinned. So I banished you in disgrace from the mountain of God. I expelled you, O mighty guardian, from your place among the stones of fire. Your heart was filled with pride because of all your beauty. Your wisdom was corrupted by your love of splendor. So I threw you to the ground and exposed you to the curious gaze of kings. You defiled your sanctuaries with your many sins and your dishonest trade. So I brought fire out from within you, and it consumed you. I reduced you to ashes on the ground in the sight of all who were watching. All who knew you are appalled at your fate. You have come to a terrible end, and you will exist no more."

Wow! Lucifer was in charge of worship in heaven. He was literally a living, breathing, sound machine of worship. Isaiah 14:11 tells us that when he lost his mind and thought he could be greater than God he stripped of everything he had been given and was cast out of heaven. "Your might and power are gone; they were buried with you. All the pleasant t music in you has ceased. Now maggots are your sheet and worms your blanket. How you are fallen from heaven, O shining star, son of the morning! You have been thrown down to the earth, you who destroyed the nations of the world. For you said to yourself, I will ascend to heaven and set my throne above God's stars. I will preside on the mountain of the gods far away in the north. I will climb to the highest heaven and be like the most High. But instead, you will be brought down to the place of the dead, down to its lowest depths. Everyone there will stare at you and ask, can this be the one who shook the earth and the kingdoms of the word? Is this the one who destroyed the world and made it into a wilderness? Is this the king who demolished the worlds' greatest cities and had no mercy on his prisoners?"

Lucifer became full of jealously of God. He thought he deserved more and strove to get more. He also thought he could compete with God. Lucifer felt that he had a right to his plan and caused division, discord, jealously and competition to run loose in heaven amongst those he lead. Don't become or allow any part of your ministry you are a part of or lead to be jealous or competitive. It will only lead to destruction. Lucifer was created to bring pleasure and delight to God through sound. When he became too full of himself he could no longer release the sound of the Lord and was cast out of His presence.

Guard your ministries and remember it is not about you but solely about God alone. Gain spiritual maturity and know who you are in God. In turn, you will walk with a humble heart-yet confident in the God in you to shine forth for others to see.

There is no need to compete. There is no need to have jealous hearts. God desires unity and oneness of hearts. He wants all of His children to come together in one accord.

Free yourself. Let the jealousy go. Let the competition go. I had to go through this process myself and I did come out on the other side. Now my heart is so full of desire to just please the Lord-however that looks. His delight is my goal now. I do all that He allows me the privilege to set my hand to for Him alone. I could care less anymore about anyone's opinions or ideals about me because I know I am firmly rooted in Christ and His love for me. It is so freeing beloved! Let it all go and walk in the freedom of unity with your fellow worshippers instead of the state of bondage and control.

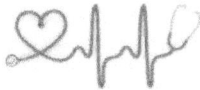

Heart Check Up

What causes you pangs of jealousy?

_____

_____

_____

♡ Who or what do you find yourself competing against either publicly or privately (or even more dangerous solely in your mind)?

_____

_____

_____

_____

♡ What seed took root in your heart for these feelings or mindsets to take root and grow?

_____

_____

_____

Ask Holy Spirit to reveal it to and then yield it to Jesus and ask Him to excavate that from your heart.

Prayer: Father, I enter your presence in the name of Jesus. Holy Spirit I am asking for you to reveal to me areas of my heart in which I have held on to jealousy and competition. I do not want to partner with these anymore and I choose to be free. Deliver me Lord from their grip. Take your fist and crush the head of the enemy in these areas of my life. Where there have been walls built of jealousy, come in like a wrecking ball and dismantle them with one blow. Where there have been divisive behaviors, come in like a wrecking ball and destroy them. Tear down every aspect and partnership with division, disunity, and the ideal of comparisons now in Jesus name. I no longer want to operate in jealousy. I want my security to be in you alone. I want my value to hold up to the plumb line of what you say about me. I no longer need to look to the left or to the right to see what I do or do not have but will solely lift and fix my eyes on you Jesus. Excavate me deep God. Rip it out. Leave no remnant behind that would bring dishonor to your name as I stand as a representative of your Kingdom. When people see me I want them to see you and nothing else. Forgive me Lord for entertaining and allowing these feelings and emotions to overrule what I know your Word says. Set me free. Deliver me. Mature me God. Mature me in your ways and align my thoughts to your thoughts. Allow me to be a vessel you can truly work through. I want to be known as one who was your lover, loved people, and moved with great power, authority and your anointing. My life should be a beacon which draws people into your Kingdom. I do not want a life that drives them away from you. In my jealous and competitive behaviors I have allowed this. I repent and receive your forgiveness. Thank you God. Thank you!

12 WORSHIP YOUR WAY WELL

"Worship your way well." This is something the Holy Spirit whispered to me on one occasion. It was in the place of intimacy and worship that I would find my healing. I had prayed my way through many trials and I had learned that worship was the only way I was going to get deeper into the heart of God in order to become well and have the ability to say "I am fully whole".

For some this may be so easy to do and not a challenge at all. To others, this may be something new for you and you may wonder how on earth do I worship my way well.

I will just share with you what Holy Spirit taught me all along the way. He taught me a lot about worship, the order of ascension into deep worship, how to enter with an expectancy to hear his response, and most importantly how to maintain fire burning on the altar of my own heart for Him.

The bible says in Leviticus 6:12-13 "Meanwhile, the fire on the altar must be kept burning; it must never go out. Each morning the priest will add fresh wood to the fire and arrange the burnt offering on it. He will then burn the fat of the peace offerings on it. Remember, the fire must be kept burning on the altar at all times. It must never go out." This scripture taught me I must be attentive and continually be in a position to have myself on the altar as a sacrifice before the Lord. Just as in the times of the Old Testament when the priests had to make sure the fire was always lit, we too today must always have a heart of burning passion for the Lord. We sacrifice our time, our personal wants, needs, and desires, and lay ourselves-our own lives-on the altar as a sacrifice to the Lord.

Another scripture the Lord used to teach me just how to build, maintain, and sustain the altar of my heart before Him was a story from 1 Kings 18:30-40. Holy Spirit taught me so much from this passage and my prayer dearest one is that you too will receive revelation for your own personal altar of your heart and experience an intimacy in worship with the King of kings which will help you as you journey down the road to worship your way well.

In 1 Kings 18:30-40 we see the account of battle of power so-to-speak. It was like a show down between gods and each side wanted to prove their god was the true God. Let's take a peek.

"Then Elijah said to them, "I am the only prophet of the LORD who is left, but Baal has 450 prophets. Now bring two bulls. The prophets of Baal may choose whichever one they wish and cut it into pieces and lay it on the wood of their altar, but **without setting fire to it**. I will prepare the other bull and lay it on the wood on the altar, **but not set fire to it** .Then call on the name of your god, and I will call on the name of the LORD. **The god who answers by setting fire to the wood is the true God!"** And all the people agreed. Then Elijah said to the prophets of Baal, "You go first, for there are many of you. Choose one of the bulls, and prepare it and call on the name of your god. But **do not set fire to the wood**." So they prepared one of the bulls and placed it on the altar. Then they called on the name of Baal from morning until noontime, shouting, "O Baal, answer us!" But there was no reply of any kind. Then they danced, hobbling around the altar they had made. About noontime Elijah began mocking them. "You'll have to shout louder," he scoffed, "for surely he is a god! Perhaps he is daydreaming, or is relieving himself. Or maybe he is away on a trip, or is asleep and needs to be wakened!" So they shouted louder, and following their normal custom, they cut themselves with knives and swords until the blood gushed out. They raved all afternoon until the time of the evening sacrifice, **but still there was no sound, no reply, and no response.**

Then Elijah called to the people, "Come over here!" They all crowded around him as **he repaired the altar of the LORD that had been torn down**. He took twelve stones, one to represent each of the tribes of Israel, and he used the stones to **rebuild the altar in the name of the LORD.** Then he dug a trench around the altar large enough to hold about three gallons. He piled wood on the altar, cut the bull into pieces, and laid the pieces on the wood. Then he said, "Fill four large jars with water, and pour the water over the offering and the wood." After they had done this, he said, "Do the same thing again!" And when they were finished, he said, "Now do it a third time!" So they did as he said, and the water ran around the altar and even filled the trench. **At the usual time for offering the evening sacrifice**, Elijah the prophet walked up to the **altar and prayed**, "O LORD, God of Abraham, Isaac, and Jacob, prove today that you are God in Israel and that I am your servant. Prove that I have done all this at your command. O LORD, answer me! Answer me so these people will know that **you, O LORD, are God** and that you have brought them back to yourself." **Immediately the fire of the LORD flashed down from heaven and burned up the young bull, the wood, the stones, and the dust.** It even licked up all the water in the trench! And when all the people saw it, **they fell face down on the ground and cried out, "The LORD—he is God! Yes, the LORD is God!"** Then Elijah commanded, "Seize all the prophets of Baal. Don't let a single one escape!" So the people seized them all, and Elijah took them down to the Kishon Valley and killed them there."

One of the first things we can see is that it was important for man to not light a fire. It was the response of God to the sacrifice set ablaze that was an important factor to show that nothing man can do in his own strength can replicate a true encounter with a holy God. It was an amazing demonstration we see take place as our God, the God who responds by fire, surely did without interference from man.

We also see here the prophets of Baal served a dead god. Elijah knew he served the living God. Evidence of a dead people with a dead god is no fire! People who serve the living God and give their lives wholly over in sacrifice to Him experience a life on fire because He is the one and only true God who does respond by fire. Others who see or surround them can see the evidence of this fire on their lives.

Elijah knew he needed to repair the altar of the Lord that was broken down in a proper manner in order for the Lord to respond. He added the extra measured of drenching the sacrifice and making a trench of water around the altar to just show even more God was THE only God and His power is infinite. It was like an amazing pyrotechnic show!

One thing that will aid in worshiping your way well is understanding your altar of worship must remain burning at all times. After you have received healing, deliverance, and freedom it is up to YOU to sustain the change.

How to you sustain the change after you have had this encounter? You must have your own altar of worship and cannot depend on another's altar to sustain the change for you. What do I mean? You cannot maintain your personal healing and deliverance if your expectation is for your pastors, leaders, mentors, worship leaders, small group, intimate group of friends, or anyone else you associate with to carry you through worship all the time. You have to sustain and maintain that change on your own. Your walk with God is yours. You cannot expect or depend someone else to carry you through all the time. Sustaining the change and the blessing which comes with it requires you to have an altar of worship in your heart.

An altar is the place where God and man meet. If you do not have a place where you regularly pray and where you seek God (sacrifice) you will not have sustained fire on your altar.

One manner to maintain an altar on fire is to die to yourself & selfish desires daily, placing God's will above your own, prayer, fasting, worship, praise, offerings, and sacrifice. Fires that go dim or go out are typically extinguished by prayerlessness, complacency, apathy, fear, trials and tribulations, problems with finances, job issues, relationship issues, etc. These types of things can stifle our ability to fully surrender on the altar because our attentions are taken away from focusing on God and they are placed on the different types of behaviors or distractions.

We must go to the altar to meet with God every day. This isn't a suggestion. It must become a daily occurrence as you realize you are nothing without Him. A desperation for His presence has to build within you on your own. I find myself running to Him every morning. I cannot begin my day without Him. When I rise in the morning, my first thoughts are on Him. I literally cannot wait to be with Him. In His presence every need is meet. In His presence every question is okay to ask and He loves to give answers to His inquisitive children. In His presence truly is fullness of joy. In His presence are warmth, love, and acceptance. Ask yourself where the fire of your first love is? Has it gone dim? Ask Him to reignite it. Elijah knew nothing would happen unless the altar was restored.

Altar is another word for closet. When you pray to the Father, close yourself in your closet. Take that time to tuck yourself away with Him. The altar is also a place of supply, strength, and where you meet with Him. There is no room for religion at all. There is only room for intimate relationship. An altar is the place of revelation and realization of change. It is in this place you also realize how much you NEED God. The glory of God illuminates our countenance and our hearts are exposed. You will see repentance take place here or your will retreat. Retreat takes places when we really do not want to see or deal with what He is showing us about ourselves. But dear one, He is not showing us these things in the secret place to bring shame or condemnation. To the contrary, He does it so that we can become more like Him.

You will not realize your own condition until you are at the altar. You begin to see God change your heart as you allow Him in to operate. There is no her fault, his fault, etc. You begin to see yourself and your condition and what needs to ultimately change.

Allow me to reiterate. You can't live off of someone else's altar. You may have mentors or a spiritual mother or father who walked you through part of your journey. Awesome! Learn from them and glean from them but you cannot rely on their altar to sustain yours. This type of relationship and holding on to their altar only works for a season of training. Jesus showed his disciples. They lived off of His altar during training, but then He said to them "I must go, but I will leave you a gift." He gave them tools to use on their own. He left the Holy Spirit who filled them with dunamis power. He basically told them 'now go with your own altars and spread the gospel.

You are responsible to cultivate your own relationship. You need to get your own bricks to build. Build your own altar for fire to be lit. Get your own worship. Activate your own prayer life. Depend on God to respond by fire.

There will be times like many of the accounts of my life personally that I shared that you may experience. When that crisis hits you, you must have your own altar to run to. You should purpose in your heart to be able to say confidently "I've prayed and I've worshipped. I have brought my own offerings and my own sacrifices to the Lord. I have tabernacle m not a stranger to Him. He responded to me and will answer me by placing fire upon my life.

We see all over the book of Act the believers gathered together, prayed together, and communed together. They created combustion or an explosion of personal altars joined together in unity and impacted thousands. They impacted all of humanity forever. That did not come from living off of someone else's altar of worship. No! It came from each one having their own personal altar of worship in the hearts and when they joined together in unity the power was magnified. The became walking tabernacles of God's presence. The lit the world on fire because they tabernacled with God, met with God regularly, walked with God daily joined God at the altar and he responded by fire.

Having a lifestyle of worship is essential. What does that look like?

You must enter His gates with thanksgiving and enter His courts with praise every day. You lay a sacrifice of yourself on the altar daily and die to your own selfish needs and wants. You allow cleansing to take place as you self-reflect and apply the Word to your life. You are in prayer with Him daily and a fragrance is released to heaven for Him to enjoy. You allow Him to illuminate areas of your heart which need to be worked on and He shines forth from you as you surrender it all to Him. Then you have community, fellowship, and enjoy daily living with Him. All of these things lead you straight to the heart of worship. They all draw you into leading a lifestyle of worship.

As you purpose to make each of these things a daily habit, you will begin to see yourself worshipping your way well. You will begin to see the reward of running to Jesus with abandon each and every day and how he so lovingly opens His arms of acceptance and allows you to jump right into the depths of His heart. This allows you to see just how vast, how immense and immeasurable His love is for you.

Build up that place for Him. Prepare it for Him. Worship your way well and watch...He will respond by fire. You will be a carrier of His fiery presence and all you come in contact with will encounter His love for them through what they see in you.

Heart Check Up

Write your personal love letter to the Lord as your first response in intimate worship to Him. Then pray your letter out loud to Him. Rebuild your altar before Him starting here.

_____

_____

_____

_____

_____

_____

_____

_____

_____

_____

13 MINISTRY

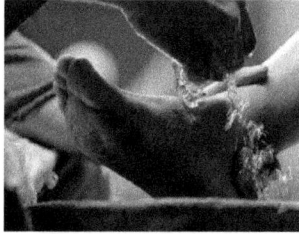

There is ministry in all of us. God gave each and every one a plan and He has a purpose for creating every single one of us. What I want to caution you about is this-Do not make ministry or ministry goals an idol in your life. When your focus is more on the ministry than on the Master you have missed it, beloved.

Allow maturation to set in along the journey as you are processed instead of rushing into anything. "Well, God told me I am going to have a big ministry and I am going to travel the world touching lives and reaching nations. I can't continue to stay small where I am. I have to move forward because the Word of the Lord came to me and I know what I am supposed to do." Ok, sounds great. Let me challenge you though. Can you even handle your household? Can you handle the pressures and stresses of your workplace? Can you handle conflict and how well do you resolve issues? Are you easily burdened or stressed? Are you easily offended? What areas of your life have you built experience and what measures have you taken to make sure you are prepared for handle the promise?

God gives us promises-yes. Some things God will give or show us to help encourage us and exhort us to keep moving forward. Not every Word of the Lord is for RIGHT NOW. There are times when He will have us wait. Oh that dreaded word WAIT in our microwave mentality today. Yes, wait. During the wait, He will process and refine you.

There are a lot of things that you will need to experience in order to prepare you for where He wants to take you. Seek Godly counsel and share your heart with trusted mentors or leaders. Even in their counsel may come a 'wait'. Don't despise them for it and feel that no one understands just how anointed you are. Really? Stay humble. Stay yielded before the Lord and do not be in a rush to be seen or known.

Find out the motive behind your need to have ministry or be the leader in a ministry and you will see whether or not your intentions are truly pure or not. Ask yourself why the draw of a platform is so enticing. Who are you doing this for- man or God?

What He promises He will fulfill. What He has shown you He will give you. Just be patient, allow the process and wait for His perfect timing and you won't have to force anything to happen.

While you are planning to run all over the place for your worldwide mission, take the time to ask when the last time you reached out to your neighbor was. When was the last time you ministered to someone who needs Jesus or who is hurting right in your own family? Don't step on people who you feel are beneath your call and anointing to get to a place to be seen and known for your own glory and then stamp God's name on it. He doesn't work that way. If you are seeking recognition or accolades-Stop right away. Take a step back and really seek God for what HE wants. If you have even the tiniest of inkling for people to approve you or applaud you, recognize it and then repent. God will lovingly redirect you and set you on your way again. Self-reflect and make sure your heart and your intentions are pure.

Ministry is not about you. Ministry is about drawing the lost to Jesus and allowing Him to ravish them with His unfailing love. Ministry is service. To serve and not be served. Ministry is a place of great humility and also great strength. Ministry puts others first and leaves self behind. Ministry is not self-seeking at all. Ministry is one of the most beautiful ways we can give ourselves back to the Lord in service to others-not ourselves.

Ministry is all about Him.

If you are ready to yield to what He wants, to His will and His way, to His design, to place yourself aside and serve, to patiently wait His perfect timing, and you are open to remaining teachable along the way THEN and only then are you ready to step out into ministry.

Always seek Him first. Always pursue Him first. Keep Him at the center at all times. His way is the best way and you will see He is faithful to all He has promised you. Just allow Him to refine you through the process so you are a vessel he surely can work through.

EPILOGUE

Most beloved reader, my prayer for you has been that in reading this book you will have been able to have an encounter with the living God and experience healing, deliverance and freedom. As you have allowed the Master Surgeon to operate on the areas of your heart that were hurt, broken, hidden and diseased, I believe you will never be the same.

May you allow the God of all creation to continue to work on you from the inside out and embrace the joys of excavation!

Go forth dear one. Go forth and be blessed as you walk out the remainder of your journey with the Lord. I pray daily, and will continue to do so, for every person whose hands have touched the pages of this book-the corridors of my heart, and whose eyes have glanced across each entry. May my story encourage, uplift, and push you to pursue the heart of the Master relentlessly and in turn receive His incredible love for you.

Be refreshed. Be renewed. Be transformed. Be healed. Be FREE!

He has created in you a clean heart and renewed a right spirit within you!

Many abundant blessings to you!

ABOUT THE AUTHOR

Reyna E. Cruz is a Pastor of Worship Arts Ministry and Founder of Break-Free Worship Arts Institute. She is passionate about worship and seeing the Arts restored to the Kingdom of God. She loves seeing others set free and ignited with this same passion and ultimately setting their own churches, ministries, homes and communities on fire and infused with power by the Holy Spirit to empower others as well.

She teaches, trains, and equips in the Word and various Art forms with a heavy concentration in several genres of dance movement both locally, regionally, and nationally. She, along with her ministry team, has also traveled to minister internationally to Nicaragua and St. Maarten.

She is a loving mother of four beautiful children and currently resides in Bethlehem, PA.

Heart Surgery Workshops/Mini Conferences

If you or someone you know are interested in inviting Reyna to speak, teach, and train in your church, ministry, small group, or event, please contact her office at bfdsoffice@gmail.com or call 610-814-7779. She is available to train in small or large settings in a workshop or conference style arena. She is also available to teach remotely.